One Soldier
and Hitler, 1918

One Soldier
and Hitler, 1918

THE STORY OF
HENRY TANDEY VC DCM MM

DAVID JOHNSON

FOREWORD BY
GENERAL LORD DANNATT GCB CBE MC DL

To Val,
and all our family.

Cover illustrations: *Front, left*: Henry Tandey in uniform with his medals. (Courtesy of the Duke of Wellington's Regiment) *Right*: Hitler in the First World War. (Wikimedia Commons) *Back*:Vickers machine-gun crew wearing anti-gas helmets, Battle of the Somme 1916. (Wikimedia Commons)

First published 2012
by Spellmount, an imprint of

The History Press
The Mill, Brimscombe Port
Stroud, Gloucestershire, GL5 2QG
www.thehistorypress.co.uk

© David Johnson, 2012

The right of David Johnson to be identified as the Author
of this work has been asserted in accordance with the
Copyrights, Designs and Patents Act 1988.

British Library Cataloguing in Publication Data.
A catalogue record for this book is available from the British Library.

ISBN 978 0 7524 6613 2

Typesetting and origination by The History Press
Printed in Great Britain

Contents

Foreword

Private Henry Tandey
VC DCM MM

Throughout my career in the Green Howards, Private Henry Tandey was always talked of in hushed tones. We all knew that he was the most highly decorated private soldier in the British Army in the First World War, but as good Green Howards we chose to ignore the fact that his principal decorations had been earned while he was serving with the Duke of Wellington's Regiment. A copy of the famous Fortunino Matania painting of Tandey carrying a wounded Green Howard comrade, surrounded by dead and dying men and horses, hung behind my desk while I was the adjutant of the 1st Battalion years later, and this perpetuated the legend about this exceptional man. Myth has it that further up the road, away from the trenches occupied by 2nd Battalion the Green Howards at the Menin Crossroads during the Battle of Ypres in 1914, and running on into the background of the painting was Adolf Hitler behind a machine gun. In that cherished belief, myth and legend reverently came together.

That is why this timely book by David Johnson is so welcome. From painstaking and detailed research, Dr Johnson has managed to winnow fact from fiction and produce the definitive life history of the remarkable British soldier who was Henry Tandey. Quite properly described as an ordinary man who did extraordinary things, he would have rubbished that description simply asserting that he was doing his duty and that if he was extraordinary at all, it was simply that he was extraordinarily lucky. That said, he would probably have used a different adjective to describe his luck, but there is no getting away from the law of averages that to survive the cauldron of the Great War with three gallantry medals, five Mentions in Despatches and three wound stripes was nothing but miraculous – of such stuff legends are indeed born.

The fascination with Henry Tandey does not end with his chestful of gallantry medals and his sleeve bereft of NCO's stripes, but takes further turns and twists that David Johnson explores with forensic diligence. The claim that a retired First World War veteran was telephoned at home in 1940 by the then prime minister, Neville Chamberlain, demands explanation. History has teased with whether Henry Tandey did in fact have Adolf Hitler in his rifle sights on 28 September 1918 near the French village of Marcoing. There is no doubt that Henry Tandey was there that day – he won the Victoria Cross on that date and in that place. There is no doubt that Hitler's regiment, the 16th Bavarian Infantry Regiment, was in the Marcoing area on that date – but was Hitler himself there? Did Neville Chamberlain, on returning from a meeting with Hitler at Berchtesgaden in 1940, telephone Henry Tandey at Hitler's request to pass on the Führer's best wishes – and was Hitler right that Tandey spared his life on 28 September 1918 by not shooting a wounded man? Such is the material with which David Johnson paints his picture of Henry Tandey – a picture albeit in a different art form, but one to rival the image of Matania's Menin Crossroads canvas.

Even though Tandey died at the age of 86 in 1977, his story was even then not complete. His medals continued the narrative after his death. Their trail runs from an auction sale in London to a mystery buyer, then to a chance encounter at a dinner party turning into a delightful relationship between the mystery buyer and Tandey's first regiment, the Green Howards, then on to a presentation of the medals in the Tower of London and finally their return to the Green Howards' home in Richmond, North Yorkshire. How all these events came about is a fascinating postscript to Tandey's life which David Johnson records with relish.

For today's young Green Howards who study the Matania painting of the Menin Crossroads, or older veterans who admire Tandey's medals in the Harrison Gallery in the Regimental Museum in Richmond, there is one final irony. The debate over whether Private Henry Tandey was a Green Howard or a hero of the Duke of Wellington's Regiment has rather run its course. Both regiments are now amalgamated and are both part of the Yorkshire Regiment, formed in 2006, so their proud histories today are one. Whether in fact Tandey would have had a strong point of view on regimental preference is now also a moot point, but it is worth recording that he was born in Leamington Spa and died in Coventry – so, he was a man of Warwickshire, not a Yorkshireman at all! Does that matter? Not at all, Henry Tandey will always be remembered as the most decorated private soldier of the First World War who, with one squeeze of the trigger, might have prevented the Second World War from starting at all. David Johnson's intriguing account is compelling to the military historian and the general reader alike. I commend it to you.

Richard Dannatt
General the Lord Dannatt GCB CBE MC DL
Chief of the General Staff 2006–9
Constable HM Tower of London

Introduction and Acknowledgements

The First World War has fascinated me since I was a young boy trying to understand what it was like to be there on the Western Front. What it must have felt like in those minutes before the whistles blew and you went over the top into what would have seemed certain death. What was it like to fix bayonets and charge the enemy? Why did they do it time after time? But it was only in 2009 that I was able to do a tour, titled 'All Quiet on the Western Front', visiting Ypres, Passchendaele, the Messines Ridge, Ploegsteert, Arras, Vimy Ridge and the Somme. Reading about those places is one thing but to actually be there was truly a powerful experience that I would recommend to anyone. Words cannot describe the effect of visiting the military cemeteries with their rows of gravestones stretching off into the distance, or indeed attending the moving ceremony held at the Menin Gate in Ypres every evening.

During the course of the tour I was struck by how many significant figures from the Second World War had served in such close proximity to each other. The list was fascinating as it included Adolf Hitler, Winston Churchill, Douglas MacArthur and Harry Truman. I have many, many books in my study on the First World

War which up until then I had read in a very general way without any particular focus or theme, but on my return I decided to study the Great War in terms of where these significant historical figures had served and what they had been involved in.

Deciding to start with Adolf Hitler, on the basis that he had served throughout the war, I read *Corporal Hitler and the Great War 1914–1918* by John F. Williams, and Ian Kershaw's book *Hitler 1889–1936 Hubris*, together with material from other sources.

Looking at information on the Internet I quite quickly came across the story of Hitler's life being spared by a British soldier at Marcoing in September 1918. That soldier was identified by Adolf Hitler as Private Henry Tandey, who between 25 August and 28 September 1918 was awarded the Military Medal, the Distinguished Conduct Medal and the Victoria Cross, becoming the most decorated private soldier to survive the war. Yet the more I read about Henry Tandey it seemed to me that he was known more for his alleged compassion towards Hitler rather than for his undoubted bravery. To me, this seemed to do him a disservice and so I decided to find out more about him, with the added interest that he was born in Leamington Spa and later lived in Coventry, while I live in Stratford-upon-Avon, so here was a local as well as a national hero.

Piecing together his life has been challenging and the research constantly threw up more questions than answers as I had to deal with, at times, the possible unreliability of memory and the inadequacies of any surviving documentation. Henry Tandey did not leave a diary or letters, or none have survived, from his time on the Western Front, there are very few remaining family members or acquaintances with any direct knowledge of him, and I was dealing largely with events that took place nearly a century ago. Nevertheless, although challenging, it has also been fascinating, as the further I delved into his life I did start to meet people who had met Henry Tandey and his second wife Annie, and I experienced too the excitement of standing in front of artefacts associated with his life and which he himself had held.

I have also come across aspects of the Great War and its aftermath that I discovered I knew little about and I have therefore included these where I think they have relevance to the life of Henry Tandey. For example, I did not know how the body of the Unknown Warrior had been selected, so I have included this because Henry Tandey played a role in the internment ceremony as one of the guard of honour in Westminster Abbey.

I have enjoyed researching the life of Henry Tandey and initially I immersed myself in the literature on the Great War and spent time reading and taking notes in my study. I did not set out to write anything about Henry Tandey but as the amount of material and information grew, I first of all entertained the possibility of writing an article. Eventually Val, my wife, suggested that I should consider writing a book and I know that I am very fortunate that The History Press were prepared to give their support to this project. Buoyed by this support, I then moved on to visiting museums, contacting Henry Tandey's family and acquaintances, and gradually building up a picture of the man and his life.

As Adolf Hitler served throughout the Great War on the Western Front, I have included limited coverage of his life up to the point where the war ended to act as a contrast to the life of Henry Tandey, but also to try to bring out some facets of his character that seem important in trying to determine whether their paths crossed in 1918. Where Hitler is concerned I have relied totally on the works of others, namely Kershaw, Williams, and Weber.

I hope that I have not written just another book on the Great War, and I certainly would not claim it to be an academic text, but hopefully it will have a broader appeal than to only military historians.

Many people have generously helped me and thanks and acknowledgements are due to the following: John Spencer (Duke of Wellington's Regimental Museum), Susan Langridge (Green Howards' Regimental Museum), Scott Flaving (Regimental Headquarters of the Yorkshire Regiment), Brian Best (Victoria Cross Society), Nigel Wilkins (Leamington Spa Picture Library), Robert Nash (Town Clerk, Leamington Spa Town Council), Denise Reynolds and Janice Williams (Henry's great nieces), Julie McDonald (Henry's great, great niece), Michael Whateley and Tony Gordon (Henry's great nephews), Henry

Gordon (nephew), Norman Parker, David Howe, Michael Crumplin FRCS, Brian Ferris (the Secretary of the Coventry (Triumph Motors) No. 4 Branch of the Royal British Legion), Peter Elkin, A. Pargetter, Jo de Vries, Chrissy McMorris and Paul Baillie-Lane (The History Press), and last but not least my wife Val.

I would also like to thank the helpful staff at the National Army Museum, the Imperial War Museum, Cadbury Research Centre at the University of Birmingham, and the Warwickshire Records Office, and I apologise to them for not having noted their names.

I am also very grateful to General the Lord Dannatt for taking the time and trouble to write the foreword to this book.

I have not yet started to look at the First World War in terms of MacArthur, Truman, and Churchill but I fully intend to and who knows what other fascinating diversions this may lead to.

In my view, the story of Henry Tandey is that of an ordinary man who, as a result of extraordinary circumstances beyond his control, performed extraordinary feats of bravery, and consequently is one I think well worth telling. He was a man described in 1918 as 'a hero of the old berserk type', and so this book is written as a tribute to him and all the other heroes from the First World War and subsequent conflicts.

I have made all reasonable efforts to ensure that the reproduction of all quotations within the pages have been included with the full consent of the copyright holders. In the event that copyright holders had not responded prior to publication, then should they so wish they are invited to contact the publishers so that any necessary corrections may be made in any future editions.

David Johnson
Summer 2012

I

An Act of Compassion Repaid?

Coventry had been subjected to intermittent bombing by the Germans since 1939, and in the September of that year the Standard Motor Works at Canley had been badly damaged, with several people injured. Perhaps surprisingly in terms of the war effort, Coventry was very much on the front line because the small factories and workshops that pre-war had been producing machine tools and car parts were now producing components vital to the conduct of the war, for instance Gardiner (2011) makes the point that three-quarters of all gauges used in the nation's armaments were made in Coventry. These factories and workshops were scattered throughout the town and could be found existing alongside historic buildings, shops and houses, so any attack on them was bound to take a toll on the civilian population and its infrastructure as well.

On the evening of Thursday 14 November 1940, what was to become known as the Coventry Blitz started at 7.20 p.m. and over the next ten hours wave after wave of German bombers dropped 500 tons of explosives, 33,000 incendiary bombs and dozens of parachute mines (Gilbert, 2008). According to the German High Command, the attack was in retaliation for the Allied bombing of Munich on 8 November.

There can be no doubt that the intention was to destroy the city and to inflict a heavy toll on its civilian population, despite the instructions issued by a German squadron leader for what was known as Operation Moonlight Sonata (Wilson, 2005):

Comrades, you are acquainted with the nature and essentials of tonight's operation. Our task is, with other squadrons, to repay the attack on Munich by the English during the night of 8th November. We shall not repay it in the same manner by smashing up harmless dwelling houses, but we shall do it in such a way that those over there will be completely stunned.

Despite those fine words, when the all clear was sounded at 6.15 a.m. the following day the horror and destruction was beyond imagination as homes, factories, public buildings and Coventry's fourteenth-century cathedral were destroyed, along with 600 lives, many too badly burned to be identified, and over 800 wounded. There were 4,330 homes destroyed, three-quarters of the city's factories damaged, and 'practically all gas and water pipes were smashed and people were advised to boil emergency supplies of water' (McGory, 2008).

One man, an air raid warden, was at home making tea for the other wardens. He told the *Sunday Graphic* what happened next:

Just as I was pouring [the tea] all hell started popping. We rushed into the street and found the whole place alight.

The ARP (Air Raid Precautions) wardens were brave men and women, and eleven of them would be killed that night.

Displaying the bravery that he had shown during the Great War, this man went to no fewer than twelve burning houses to rescue the trapped occupants. In many cases he had to fight his way through the flames to rescue the half-suffocated women and children who had been trapped in their cellars, only to find later that his own home, in Cope Street, had been destroyed. The casualty figures would have been worse if the authorities had not provided some seventy-nine public bunkers that could house up to 33,000 people (Gardiner), where in very cramped conditions children were frightened and in some cases hysterical, women sobbed and everyone was scared.

As he stood in front of his home that had been reduced to rubble, he would have felt a number of understandable emotions, and he would almost certainly have thought about the news that he had received the year before. According to what he had been told he had once had the opportunity to kill the man responsible for all the death and destruction that he saw around him.

Standing there surrounded by the decimation of the town in which he lived, he would have watched the flames licking the sky as they consumed the cathedral – the only one in Britain to be destroyed in the war. Morning brought with it the acrid smell of smoke and burning, and a blood-red sky. He would have seen people wandering about in a state of shock with their eyes red and sore from the effects of the smoke, searching for friends and relatives, and staring in utter disbelief at what was left of their property and the city's landmarks. He would have seen the dead and wounded being removed from the ruins, and heard the moans and screams.

It is possible that on the following day he, along with others, would have drawn some consolation from the visit of King George VI, who spent time seeing for himself areas of the devastated city. Perhaps he went to see the King walking through the rubble, broken glass and other debris, who through his visit was making an effort to raise morale, and he would have remembered, perhaps, the time he had met the King's father, George V, soon after the end of the previous world war.

Perhaps as he stood watching the King he was holding the one thing he had been able to retrieve from his devastated home, a clock that had been presented to him by the Old Contemptibles' Association in April 1920. On the back of the clock was an inscription which read:

L/Cpl Tandey VC, DCM, MM, Duke of Wellington's Regiment, Old Contemptibles' Association, as a token of esteem and comradeship, April 1920.

This man, who was slight of stature, short and ram-rod straight, was indeed Henry Tandey VC DCM MM (Victoria Cross, Distinguished Conduct Medal, and Military Medal), who was the most highly decorated private soldier to have survived the First World War.

Nothing on the scale of this bombing and devastation had been experienced in Britain before and his thoughts, assailed by these horrors, would have gone back to an incident twenty-two years before when he had apparently been given the opportunity to change history and spare the misery that he saw all around him. In August 1939 he had discovered that he had been named by Adolf Hitler as the British soldier who had spared the German Führer's life in September 1918. He was said to have aimed his rifle at a wounded and retreating German soldier, and in an act of compassion decided not to shoot. He would surely have reflected on how that act of compassion had been repaid.

That Britain's most decorated private soldier spared the life of Adolf Hitler makes for a great story accepted by some and disputed by many others. It is a story where the truth may never be absolutely known, if only because its participants are all now dead, but it is impossible to write a biography of Henry Tandey without addressing this issue.

2

The Early Years

According to his birth certificate, Henry John Tandey was born on 30 August 1891 in Swains Buildings, Kenilworth Street, Leamington Spa, in Warwickshire. His birth was registered, no doubt, under the watchful gaze of the Registrar E. Ainsworth on 8 October 1891, by his mother Catherine who gave her address at the time as 2 Albion Row, Leamington Spa. His parents were James Tandey (1869–1944) and Catherine Tandey (1873–1946), who had married on 5 January 1891 at the parish church in Leamington Priors.

James Tandey was a well-known figure around Leamington Spa who was treated with caution by others due to his temper, and in particular his tendency to brawl following a drinking session. It was rumoured that as a young man he had received a kick to the head from a horse, and that this had an adverse effect on his character and personality. He was certainly not a man to get on the wrong side of and his reputation preceded him.

Catherine was from Ireland but had come to England with a sister and their mother, Jane Conroy, and she was to be the cause of a major disagreement between James Tandey and his father. The Tandeys were a wealthy family and his father considered that James was marrying beneath him. This disagreement resulted in James disowning his father and petulantly changing his family name to 'Tandy'. It seems likely that Catherine was pregnant with Henry at the time of their marriage, which would have added to the family tension.

As a result, Henry was baptised at St Peter's Roman Catholic Church on 11 September 1892 under the name Henricus Joannes Tandy. On both his birth certificate and his entry in the baptism register Henry's surname is spelt 'Tandy', but as soon as he was able he made the decision to revert to spelling his name 'Tandey'. Henry's decision to return to 'Tandey' reflects the fact that he had his own issues with his father, although none of his siblings chose to follow his lead. This act by Henry was just one of the manifestations of inter-generational family conflict, and indeed sibling conflict, that would persist through later generations as well.

The spelling of Henry's surname has caused some confusion, as, for example, the *London Gazette*'s citation for Henry's Victoria Cross spelt his surname as 'Tandey' yet for the Military Medal it was spelt 'Tandy'. On Henry's medal records there is one card in the name of Tandy, which has a handwritten note which says 'See Tandey', and another in the name of Tandey which says 'See Tandy'.

Where there are surviving letters from Henry, all written in later life, they are signed 'Tandey' and so, for the purposes of this book, the spelling that will be used is 'Tandey', except for when it was spelt in the alternative form in any original quotations or documents referred to.

★★★

Henry was born into a world of gaslights, trams, and cinemas showing silent, black-and-white films accompanied by live musicians. In 1902 a free library had opened in Leamington Spa where people were not allowed to browse or touch the books. Anyone wanting a book had to place a request via a librarian. Books were to be treated as rare and precious objects, usually always hardback copies, because they would not have been subjected to the large print runs of modern times.

Until 1896 the law required vehicles propelled by steam, petrol or electricity to be proceeded by a man on foot carrying a red flag (Howe, 2004), and it was five years after Henry had been born that the motorcar made its first public appearance at the Crystal Palace Exhibition (Wilson, 2005). However, by 1913 some 33,800 had been purchased, and by 1910 fatal accidents involving cars outnumbered those involving horse-drawn vehicles.

Living in the twenty-first century it is hard to envisage a life without cars but a look at the photograph of the Regent Hotel, Leamington Spa (plate 4), taken in about 1880, shows the Parade with no more than three horse-drawn carriages, and a street sweeper and his cart in the middle of the street. A photograph taken today would look somewhat different, and anyone standing in the middle of the street would at best be unpopular and at worst in danger from the passing cars, buses and delivery vehicles.

Saltzman (1951) stated that Leamington Spa had not been particularly noted for anything until the early nineteenth century, when it had started to be developed as a spa town. Interest in the town as a spa steadily increased with more and more people coming to take the waters, including royalty. One royal visitor was Princess Victoria, who in 1838, as Queen Victoria, granted the town the right to style itself 'Royal' Leamington Spa.

★★★

Henry was born into a military family, and was sometimes known as Harry or 'Napper', although the origins of the nickname are not known. Henry's father, James, served in the 16th Lancers (Smith, 2001), taking part in the fighting in South Africa, and he was also called up as a reservist in the Great War.

The 16th Lancers were deployed to fight in the Boer War in 1900, returning to England in 1904 having fought at the Battles of Paardeberg and Diamond Hill, and played a leading role in the relief of Kimberley.

In February 1900 the 16th Lancers were moving towards Kimberley, and James Tandy would have endured experiences that his son Henry would come to recognise in the Great War, as can be seen from the diary entry of Captain R. W.D. Bellew (Carver, 2000):

> Up at daylight again, and moved N of Kimberley no water or feed horses in desperate state were sent out as advanced squadron and came under the hottest fire we've yet had while cutting wire had to retire fortunately only 4 horses hit. Got back after dark.

From March to May 1900, the 16th Lancers were involved in fighting around Bloemfontein, and the story can again be picked up from Captain Bellew's diary entries:

> 7th March
> Heard guns early and saw main body disappearing over horizon turning position on enemy's left. Saw them leave kopje hill and finally they left Table kopje to our front without firing a single shot as infantry threatened on their right. We at once advanced and occupied Table kopje from which we had glorious view for a long time of the whole movement. Enemy retired as fast as they could get their wagons away while cavalry swept round on the right and infantry pressed them back on the left. Towards evening bivouacked beyond Boer's furthest position.
> 8th
> Halted all day to rest horses and get up forage ... Yesterday was completely successful though there was not much firing and very few casualties on either side.

Henry would certainly come to experience the confusion of battle, and would have recognised the following entry in Captain Bellew's diary for 31 March:

> At 11.30 orders came to turn out at once and repulse attack by somebody somewhere. All horses were out grazing and the men scattered about washing etc. After some confusion the regiment managed to produce 4 full troops.

It is quite possible that on his return James would, through his stories, have encouraged Henry and his brothers to consider military life, as Henry's brothers James and Samuel would also serve in the Great War, with Samuel being wounded at the Battle of Jutland (Smith, 2001).

Henry's father was also a stonemason/journeyman, and his grandfather, also James, of Norfolk Street, Leamington Spa, was a reputable and well-respected marble mason who, at times, worked for George Gilbert Scott, an architect who is best known for the Albert Memorial and the Midland Grand Hotel at St Pancras railway station in London. It is likely therefore that the Tandey family originally came to Leamington Spa to find work, attracted by the amount of building taking place associated with the town's development at that time, but there is no evidence that Henry ever wanted to follow this family profession.

★★★

At the age of 5, Henry became a pupil at St Peter's School for Boys in New Street, which was founded in 1848 and closed in 1967. By the time Henry started his education it was free and pupils' attendance no longer depended on their parents' ability to pay the daily fee of 1d. Henry would have remained there until 1905, when the school leaving age was by then 14, as a result of the 1902 Education Act. In the absence of reliable, or indeed any, records, it is not clear whether Henry attended the school for all or some of the period from 1901–05 for reasons that will be discussed later, although there is a school photograph taken in about 1905 (plate 3), where he certainly looks more than happy.

Henry's lessons would have focused on reading, writing and arithmetic. There are no school records relating to Henry but a picture of his schooldays can be built up through the work of O'Shaugnessy (1979), who gives an insight into how education was conducted at this time based on learning by rote:

Tables were chanted every morning from the blackboard, passages from the Bible and mournful poems were memorised and 'said out loud' in unison. Dreary lists of spellings, each broken up into syllables, were repeated exhaustingly. Even sums were gone over on the blackboard, the whole class intoning the phrases.

Children took turns to read out loud to the class and any lapses were diligently corrected by the teacher. It must have come as a relief to the pupils when schools acquired more books, allowing each child the opportunity to select one in which they might have some genuine interest and also adopt silent reading, perhaps as a reward for flawlessly reading aloud.

Even if he was not punished himself, Henry would have witnessed how discipline was maintained through the use of the cane. The cane was not only used to deal with misbehaviour, but also for:

> Bad writing or an unfortunate inability to do arithmetic. If a child came to school dirty or late, because a slatternly mother had failed him, he was caned. If he dropped a blot on to his exercise book from his atrocious pen or sited his sums on the wrong side of the page, if his sister dirtied the hard calico she was endeavouring to stitch – Nemesis was waiting.

While it is easy to be critical of the use of corporal punishment it needs to be remembered that times were different then and this form of discipline was seen as acceptable in dealing with classes in excess of fifty pupils. It may also be the case that the discipline Henry experienced in school stood him in good stead when he later joined the army, which had similar approaches to discipline and conformity.

★★★

In the early 1800s, Roman Catholics in Leamington Spa had at first worshipped in a large room in Clemens Street, but in 1828 they had built their own church in George Street, and then in 1864 moved to the present St Peter's church in Dormer Place. This church, except for the tower which had been put up in 1878, was burnt down in 1883, but was rebuilt in red brick with stone dressings in 1884 (Saltzman).

In her book, O'Shaugnessy states that:

> The children in Roman Catholic Schools were amongst the poorest and most deprived of the town, living in slum dwellings, ill-clothed, and inadequately fed. Suffering from malnutrition, these children were sadly lethargic in body and mind, and were prey to illnesses and complaints of all kinds.
>
> Generous Catholics provided clothing and shoes and gifts of food for the children and organised Christmas treats and summer outings, but the home conditions continued.

According to the parish historian of St Peter's, the Tandey family attended church each week, and it is likely that they were among the generous Catholics who made donations.

***

By the time of the 1901 census, the world was changing. Edward VII became king on 22 January following the death of Queen Victoria; the Commonwealth of Australia was inaugurated on 1 January; the Boer War was being fought in South Africa; and on 12 December Marconi was responsible for the first wireless signal to be transmitted across the Atlantic.

The census records for 1901 showed that the Tandy family was living at 178 Warneford Terrace, and that the household comprised Henry's mother, Catherine, who was recorded as working as a laundress aged 30, Henry, two further sons, James and Samuel (aged 7 and 1), a daughter aged 4, and their grandmother Jane Conroy who was 82.

It was Catherine who was recorded as the head of the household, not James, and his absence has led to much speculation that there were problems in Henry's parents' marriage that had led them to separate or divorce. There is no evidence for this being the case in 1901, and James' absence from the family home at the time of the census almost certainly reflected the fact that he was away serving in the army in South Africa. The head of each household, then as now, was given a census form to fill in on behalf of everyone residing in the household on a certain date, so there was no way that James could be recorded as living at the family home.

In fact, the 1911 census, conducted the year after Henry had joined the army, showed James as the head of the household and his occupation was shown as a 'monumental mason'. It also showed Catherine, who by now was not working, and four children. The children were Magdeline (known to the family as Madeline or Madge), aged 15 having been born in 1896, who was employed as a bookbinder; Florence, aged 7 (b. in 1904); Robert aged 5 (b. 1906); and George, aged 10 months (b. 1911). By this time the family was living at 19 Kenilworth Street, Leamington Spa, in a five-room house. The census record showed that by 1911, the children's grandmother, Jane Conroy, was dead, and that Catherine had given birth to eight children, of whom seven had survived. By 1911, Henry was already in the army but there is no record of the whereabouts of James, who would by then have been 17, or Samuel, who would have been 11. Two further sons, Frederick and Edward, were born sometime after 1911.

★★★

According to information that Henry supplied to the Victoria Cross Society, he had spent some time in an orphanage, but the circumstances that led to this are not known. It has not been possible from the existing archive records to establish the truth of this or the reasons, dates or name of the orphanage concerned. The parish historian of St Peter's Church can find no records of an orphanage attached to the church, and the existing members of the family can shed no light on this either. Henry's nephew, Henry Gordon, who at the time of writing was aged 95 and will feature later in this book, has no knowledge of him being placed in an orphanage. Nevertheless, according to Henry he did spend some time in one and, therefore, it cannot be ignored and as such, where this book is concerned, it perhaps comes under the heading of an 'inconvenient truth'.

A search at the Warwickshire Records Office revealed no references for any orphanages in Leamington Spa, but in *Kelly's Directory* for 1904, under 'Homes', there was one for the Leamington area. This was the St Michael's Home, run by the sisters of the Community of St John the Baptist, in 23 Charlotte Street, but it was a Church of England establishment and, given that the Tandys were Roman Catholics, it is unlikely that Henry was placed there.

There is no reason to think that Henry lied about this stage of his life, and it would indeed be a strange thing to lie about, but the absence of definitive records can only lead to speculation on the matter. The absence of any orphanages could mean that Henry was instead placed in a private home. There is evidence that by the time of his death in 1924 James Tandy was a wealthy man, but whether he had acquired his wealth by this time and therefore paid for Henry to be placed in a private home is not known. It could be that Henry was a disruptive youth who fell foul of the law and ended up in a reformatory, but again there are no records available for examination, and he does not seem to have been that type of boy or young man. Henry Gordon remembers the Tandys, including his mother Magdeline, as a closed group when it came to talking about the family history, and so if it had happened then no one spoke about it.

It is possible that Henry actually found himself in a workhouse, where the children were separated from the adult occupants. If this was the case then Henry almost certainly would have entered the Warwick Union Workhouse. This was located in Lakin Road, on what is now the site of Warwick Hospital. Henry may have found it more socially acceptable to admit in later life to a stay in an orphanage rather than a workhouse, because of the stigma attached to the latter.

The 1901 census records show that Henry was recorded as part of the family household when he was 10 years of age. Children had to leave the workhouse no later than their sixteenth birthday, which in Henry's case would have been 1907, or be transferred to the male, adult section, so this particular episode in his life occurred for all, or some of, the period 1901 to 1909. It is unlikely, therefore, that while Henry was in the workhouse he would have been able to continue as a pupil at St Peter's School for Boys in Leamington Spa due to the distance involved, and yet the school photograph taken *c.* 1905 shows a happy, smiling boy, so the mystery deepens.

It is also a possibility that he was joined there for some or all of the time by his brothers James and Samuel, who, as was noted above, were not living in the family home at the time of the census in 1911.

If Henry did spend time in an orphanage or workhouse then it is not possible to know how he felt about this period of his life, but it is arguable, with hindsight (although Henry may not have felt so at the time), that it probably had a positive effect in terms of the discipline it would have instilled where both his civilian jobs and military service were concerned.

★★★

At the age of 18 in 1909, Henry went to work at the Regent Hotel in Leamington Spa as a stoker, and later as an assistant engineer, where his duties involved stoking the boilers and supervising the machinery in the hotel's laundry. The hotel had been built and opened in 1819 and was initially called the Williams Hotel, but its name later changed to the Regent Hotel in honour of Albert the Prince Regent.

As discussed above, Henry would have had to leave any workhouse at 16 or alternatively be transferred to the male, adult section of the workhouse that he was in. If this was the case then there is no information available as to what he did in the two years before he went to work at the Regent Hotel. The options are that he remained in the workhouse until 1909, before he left it to take up undisclosed employment, or it may be possible that he went to work with his father or grandfather for a time.

An article in the spring issue (1981) of *This England* described Henry as being an all-round sportsman in his youth. A schoolboy friend, Fred Steane of the Hampton Dairy, Regent Street, Leamington

Spa, recalled in the *Leamington Morning News* on 2 August 1976 that he and Henry had played for the same football team. Given Henry's size and stature, 5ft 5in and 119lb, it is most likely that he played either as a fullback or winger. No further information is available about Henry and sport but he is likely to have also enjoyed athletics and would of, in all likelihood, participated in events at the Jephson Gardens, in Leamington Spa, among other places.

***

James Tandey, Henry's grandfather, had become a wealthy man and this produced a further and final manifestation of the problems that existed between father and grandfather. Henry's grandfather marked his continued displeasure with his son James by drawing up a will on 6 November 1923, in which he proposed to leave ten houses, his workshops and stone yard to his daughters from a second marriage. The will details the wealth that had been accrued, including furniture such as a black and gilt sideboard, an inlaid marble table, a marble clock, a sideboard with glass fronts and some property located at Midhurst in Sussex as well as in Leamington Spa. His eldest daughter, Kate Oldham, would inherit the bulk of the estate, while her three sisters would also receive property in the town. The workshops and the stone yard were to be left to a grandson, Reginald Charles Eagles.

Henry's father, who would have had expectations of receiving a substantial part of the inheritance, discovered that he was to be left the interest on an invested sum of £200, as detailed in the will:

To my son James Tandey I leave two hundred pounds to be invested for his life only and the interest of the two hundred pounds to be paid to him weekly by my daughter Kate Oldham. At the death of my son James Tandey I wish it to be given to my grandchildren. Twenty five pounds to Harry Tandey VC, fifty pounds to Fred Tandey or his survivors, twenty five pounds to Sam Tandey of Hull, fifty pounds to Florrie Tandey and fifty pounds to Frederick Evans son of Ellen Eliza Evans.

James felt humiliated enough by the bulk of the estate going to his father's daughters, but this was further compounded by the stipulation that the money left to him was to be invested and then paid to him in weekly instalments by his sister Kate.

Henry's grandfather died in 1924.

★★★

In August 1910, Henry had joined the army with ideas, no doubt, of adventure and travel possibly fuelled, as speculated earlier, by tales from his father's military service. But also, in all probability, to escape from a job which at various times would have been back breaking, dirty and almost certainly tedious – and also, quite possibly, from his family situation.

HITLER'S EARLY YEARS

It is not the purpose of this book to give a detailed examination of Adolf Hitler's life, those interested in the detail can turn to the more eminent works of Kershaw, Williams and Weber. An examination of Hitler's life is only used in this book as a contrast to Henry's life, and to help to unravel their alleged connection.

In giving an overview of Hitler's life before joining the army, it would be too complicated to refer to him just by his family name, and so up until 1914, when he joined the army, he will be referred to by his first name of Adolf.

Adolf Hitler was born on 20 April 1889 in a small Austrian town called Braunau, near to the German border, and he too appears to have had a troubled upbringing. The family name was originally Schicklgruber, which was changed to the more familiar Hitler in 1876. Adolf's father, Alois, had had a difficult childhood as he was an illegitimate child, and the name of his father has never been established, although many versions of who and why have been bandied about.

Alois, despite an unremarkable academic background, rose from being a junior-grade civil servant in the Austrian Ministry of Finance to a customs inspector, and finally, in 1892, he became a Higher Collector of Customs in Passau. Alois had a colourful private life and Adolf's mother, Klara, was to be his third wife, with the three marriages producing a total of nine children.

In 1873, Alois had married Anne Glassl, but in 1880 she had been granted a legal separation due to his affair with Franziska Matzelberger. At this time wife number three to be, Klara Polzl, was working as a maid in Alois' household but Franziska, mindful of Alois and his roving eye, demanded that she be sent away. Franziska died in 1884 and, needing someone to help with the household, in particular the two children of that relationship, Alois brought Klara back who then became pregnant, leading to their marriage in 1885.

Alois Hitler's work necessitated the family moving many times when Adolf was growing up. Adolf Hitler was the fourth of six children from this marriage but his older siblings, Gustav, Ida and Otto, died when they were very young. The two younger siblings were Edmund and Paula. Kershaw (1998) argues that despite Adolf's later claims to the contrary, the family 'led a comfortable middle class existence'.

Adolf's father had a bad temper that could quickly flare up and his children, including Adolf and possibly his mother, experienced the results of this. He also had no real affection for or interest in bringing up his family and so that was left to Klara. Consequently, Klara was adored by Adolf who later stated in *Mein Kampf* (Kershaw) that 'I honoured my father but loved my mother'.

In 1895 the family moved to Lambach, and on 1 May Adolf started at primary school where he achieved 'high marks for school work and behaviour'. Several things then happened that must have produced an element of instability in Adolf's life, including further house moves and his father's retirement in 1895. One family move was to Linz in 1898, which Adolf from then on viewed as his home town.

It was in 1898 that Adolf started secondary school and the already difficult relationship with his father worsened, as Alois' plan was for him to become a civil servant and consequently he had selected a *realschule* for Adolf's secondary education. The *realschule*, in contrast to a *gymnasium*, attached less importance to 'traditional classical and humanistic studies' (Kershaw), favouring instead modern subjects such as science and technical studies. From this point on Adolf's behaviour and attainment started to become problematical.

Kershaw speculates that this could have been Adolf's way of sabotaging his father's plans. If he did decide to hide his true abilities and condition then it reveals the first evidence of a trait because, as will be discussed later, he seemed to have adopted the same tactic to avoid conscription into the Austrian Army.

While at secondary school, a class mate described him as 'stubborn, high-handed, dogmatic, and hot tempered' (Kershaw), and in that respect he seems to have shared many of his father's traits.

It was at this time that he announced to his father that he intended to become an artist. It is not possible to say with certainty how this news was received, but given Alois' temperament it is not likely to have been well received. Almost certainly to Adolf's relief, therefore, his father died in 1903, ending the pressure felt from that source. Due to his lack of good behaviour and attainment, Adolf left his *realschule* for another, 50 miles away, and as a result had his first experience of living away from home, which he seems not to have enjoyed. In all likelihood he did not enjoy the separation from his much-loved mother and a home where all his needs were catered for.

Initially, Adolf seemed to do better at his new school but he was not happy and seems to have resorted to his tried and trusted strategy of pretence, this time convincing his mother that he was simply too ill to continue there. Adolf therefore left his school without securing his leaving certificate.

Klara died in December 1907, by which time Adolf was enjoying a fairly casual lifestyle attending the theatre and opera in Vienna. In 1906, he persuaded Klara to pay for him to visit Vienna, staying there for two weeks (Kershaw), and he returned with the idea of gaining a place at the Vienna Academy of Fine Arts. By this time it became clear that his mother was very ill with a terminal cancer, but nevertheless he returned to Vienna in September 1907, though he failed to pass the academy's entrance examination.

Undeterred, Adolf decided to re-apply in 1908 but then came his mother's death and such was his attachment to his mother that it must have been a traumatic moment in his life. He returned to Vienna in February 1908, claiming in later life that he had not been left with the means of supporting himself. He had seen, he said, what money Alois had left spent on his mother's nursing care, leaving him with just an orphan's pension. Kershaw disputes this and argues that Adolf did have sufficient funds, and there is no evidence that he sought to change his lifestyle.

The academy did not allow Adolf a second opportunity to take the entrance examination and without a leaving certificate he also could not apply to his next option, the School of Architecture. Despite this he chose to spend the remaining years leading up to the outbreak of the Great War living in Vienna, and, by 1909, he was virtually living as a down and out. With both of his parents dead and his inheritance spent, he made some sort of a living by performing odd jobs, painting picture postcards or designing adverts for local businesses. Furthermore, his aspirations to be an artist had been shattered by his two rejections from the Viennese Academy of Art. At night he slept in a doss-house behind a railway station (Bullock), moving to a hostel for men, where he lived from 1910–13.

★★★

At this stage of their respective stories there are a number of interesting similarities; both Henry and Adolf came from large and troubled families, where neither seem to have enjoyed a positive relationship with his father. Both were baptised into the Roman Catholic faith but it was only in Henry's case that this was to remain an important facet throughout his life.

At this stage of their lives Henry was a worker whilst Adolf was more of a dreamer who wanted, but ultimately failed, to be an artist. Henry chose to join the army in 1910 but Adolf would only join up at the outbreak of the war in 1914.

While the above observations may or may not be interesting, there are two salient points which emerge from this brief overview, namely that Adolf was prepared to resort to pretence to achieve his ends, and that he was prepared to state a different version of reality when it suited him. He lived in what Kershaw describes as an 'egoistic fantasy world', a point that will be returned to later.

3

Military Service

1914

Henry either did not keep a diary or it has not survived, nor are there any letters to provide a record of his thoughts, feelings, observations and experiences of the First World War. Researching Henry's military service is also hampered by the fact that although all soldiers had a personal file, according to the National Archives only about 40 per cent survived following the German air raid on London on the night of 7/8 September 1940.

However, it is not unreasonable to assume that he would have been like any other soldier, excited at the prospect of going to war, certain it would be over quickly and perhaps understandably nervous as well. In the absence of any documents relaying Henry's own words, Henry's military life will be looked at through the recorded experiences of others, because how they felt and what they experienced in all likelihood would have applied to Henry. If those soldiers in a trench or under fire felt afraid, cold, dirty, lice-ridden and hungry then Henry's experience is unlikely to have been any different.

Henry was a Warwickshire man, yet on joining the army he found himself assigned to the Alexandra Princess of Wales' Own Yorkshire Regiment (19th Foot), later known as the Green Howards, as Private Tandey No. 9545, on the basis that this regiment had vacancies to fill. He served with the 2nd Battalion in South Africa and Guernsey, and as a servant to Captain Chauncey.

The regimental website of the Green Howards shows that the regiment had been formed in 1688, and following the prevailing convention that regiments took the name of their colonel, it was known as the Howards. As the regimental uniform had green facings, it was known informally in 1774 as the Green Howards, a nickname that stuck, to differentiate it from the Buff Howards. In 1875 the regiment had been presented with new colours by Alexandra the Princess of Wales, at which point the regiment had taken the name the Princess of Wales' Own. Nevertheless, the nickname stuck and in 1920 the regiment became officially known as the Green Howards.

Henry weighed 119lb and was 5ft 5in in height at a time when volunteers had to be at least 5ft 3in, so he was not particularly small in stature by army standards at that time. He was remembered by his friend Cecil Bacon, who served with him in the Green Howards, as a fine, upstanding young man, who instilled confidence in those around him. These would be the qualities that he would demonstrate throughout his military career.

A battalion was formed of thirty-five officers and a thousand men who were divided into four companies (about 240 men), sixteen platoons (of sixty men) and sixty-four sections (of fourteen men), and was of a size that meant Henry would have known the other members of the battalion at least by sight if not by name, as it was not so big as to make it impersonal.

At the outbreak of the First World War the battalion returned to England from Guernsey, arriving at Southampton on 28 August 1914, where it was attached to the 21st Brigade, 7th Division.

Early in October, after a period of training, the troops left their New Forest camp in Hampshire early in the morning and set off for embarkation at Southampton, where they were met by thousands of people along the route cheering and waving. Slowly but surely the men would have responded by straightening up as they marched, sticking out their chests and occasionally waving back if they spotted a pretty face. After all, this war would be over by Christmas so what was there to be down about?

★★★

The men wore a uniform that had been developed in 1902 and was known as Service Dress (Doyle, 2010):

> Its tunic was loose fitting, with a turned down collar, patches at the shoulder to bear the extra wear from the position of the rifle butt in action, and four pockets with button down flaps.

On their heads the men were wearing a khaki peaked cap, although in late 1914 they would be issued with a softer winter trench cap with flaps that could be fastened under the chin to provide some protection to the ears and face from the cold weather. The 'softer' hats gave no real protection against a bullet or shrapnel, leading to a prevalence of head injuries, and it wasn't until 1916 that Henry was issued with a steel helmet.

Their trousers had narrow legs and were worn with puttees and woollen socks. Puttees provided support to the lower leg but if tied too tightly they could restrict the blood supply to the legs, which was a major contributory factor, when combined with moving around in the wet environs of the Western Front, to the condition known as trench foot.

Many soldiers succumbed to trench foot in the later stages of 1914 because of the poor drainage and lengthy exposure to damp and cold conditions in the trenches. It was a fungal infection of the feet, causing them to swell up. The soldiers' feet were numbed by the cold and wet, but as their feet warmed up they would experience tremendous pain, and in severe cases gangrene would set in, leading to amputation of the toes.

Trench foot became less of a problem when the army made the local commanders accountable for any outbreaks, thereby forcing them to improve trench conditions by the provision, whenever possible, of dry standing, the use of pumps when these were available, and regular feet inspections. The men were encouraged to keep their feet dry, their toes greased and to change their socks every day.

The uniform was completed by a pair of regulation field boots made of thick leather and soles covered in metal studs, which would have been unsuitable for marching on cobbled or other hard road surfaces. Very few men would have avoided blisters (caused by friction) or calluses (caused by pressure) no matter what preventative measures were tried such as soaping the feet before marching to reduce friction, wearing two pairs of socks, not removing boots until their feet had cooled down, or soaking them until any swelling had gone down (Winter, 1979).

But as the war progressed variations to the uniform, both official and unofficial, would be introduced.

Henry would have carried a Short Magazine Lee-Enfield (SMLE) rifle with ammunition clips holding five bullets, and the rifle magazine holding another ten bullets. Gradually through history the length of the rifle barrel had been shortened and so, as well as his rifle, Henry would have carried a 17in bayonet to give the necessary reach to deal with the longer-length rifles of the German soldiers.

In addition to his rifle, Henry would have used grenades which needed no particular skill to use. These were, at first, unwieldy 16in stick grenades, which were replaced by what was known as the 'jam tin'. This was a tin packed with explosive gun cotton and shrapnel balls, which was replaced in 1915 by the Mills grenade; this was activated by the removal of a pin prior to being thrown in the direction of the enemy.

Each soldier would have worn a system of webbing made up of a belt, cross straps, cartridge carriers, water bottle, entrenching tool and bayonet carrier, together with some form of haversack.

★★★

Henry and his fellow soldiers boarded their ships at Southampton and then set sail for Dover, where, inexplicably, they found themselves riding at anchor for the best part of a day while the army sorted out where to send them. The original plan had been to send the 7th Division to Antwerp but, with the Belgian Army in retreat and the city about to fall to the Germans, the decision was made to land on the Mole at Zeebrugge. The 7th Division was under the command of Major General Capper, and as his men landed only he would have realised that the men of that division represented the last remaining reserves of the regular army.

On 6 October 1914 Henry landed at Zeebrugge to join up with the British Expeditionary Force (BEF), and was soon deployed to wait for the arrival of the by now much-depleted and retreating BEF at Ypres, and such was the rush to get the division in place that it used whatever transport was available, including lorries, buses and private cars. From the British perspective, holding Ypres was vital given its proximity to the Channel coast. If the Germans had taken it, the BEF would have been cut off from the coast and the war would have been virtually over almost before it had begun.

Corns and Hughes-Wilson (2001) make the point that the British Army, of which Henry had been a part of since 1910, had 'experienced a war of manoeuvre, and prided itself on its battle readiness', but it was ill prepared for the war it now faced, lacking 'reserve manpower, heavy artillery, and an industrial base geared for the mass production of ammunition'. It was to be a form of war that, quite simply, had not been planned for. This was the situation that Henry faced as he found himself in Ypres.

The division arrived at Ypres on 14 October, a week after the town had been virtually ransacked by the Germans. The town had enjoyed great prosperity as a medieval cloth town, although over the years its importance had diminished. Ypres, sitting on the very flat Flanders plain, had a succession of low hills to the north and north-east, and was a town that was dominated by its grand Gothic Cloth hall, which was soon to be destroyed. As it developed into the Ypres Salient this area would become notorious as a killing ground for those living and fighting there.

Lieutenant J.D. Wyatt of the 2nd Battalion noted in his diary on 7 December the repercussions on the local population of the war going on around them (Brown, 2001):

> A lot of houses are being demolished by our engineers to clear the 'field of fire' for our guns. It is heartbreaking to see old women trundling a barrow away with the few things she can save in it. Then our fellows go and blow her house up. War is awful for civilians. Far worse for them than for us. May England never be the seat of conflict.

The division took part in the First Battle of Ypres, suffering heavy losses, after which it became known as the 'Immortal Seventh'. Henry and his battalion were at Petit Kruiseke on 15 October for the battle's opening shots and a successful action was fought on the Broodseinde Ridge from 19–21 October, which not only held up but also inflicted heavy casualties on the Germans. The division stayed at Ypres, fighting near Gheluvelt, Kruiseke Hill and Zillebeke.

Although, as has been said, there are no diaries or letters of Henry's from the Western Front, the Imperial War Museum's file on him contains an unidentified newspaper cutting (it has not been possible to identify the newspaper concerned despite approaching the British Library and the National Media Museum) of a feature column titled 'Answers', dated 23 September 1939, in which Henry talks about the fighting at the Menin Crossroads:

> We had no trenches. We were lying in shallow holes scooped out of the sand, often a hundred yards apart, and no way of getting back. The nearest rations had been dumped a mile and a half behind us and the only way of getting them was to crawl up the ditch beside the Ypres

Road. When we were thirsty we stretched our handkerchiefs over the mud in the corner of the trench and sucked.

Henry and his comrades had no idea of the situation that faced them but over the succeeding hours, as more and more troops retreated through their lines, its seriousness became apparent:

It was touch and go for four days. They were attacking all the time, and our barbed wire, raided from the farm fences and fitted with tin cans containing pebbles to act as alarm signals, wasn't much protection.

As the number of casualties grew, the troops had other problems to contend with, as Henry recalls the farm livestock that had been left behind as the civilian population had left their homes. The troops did their best for these animals and, despite being under fire, managed to turn the cattle loose, but they continued to return to their byres, where many were killed by rifle and artillery fire. It seems, though, that Henry and his comrades had far more trouble with the pigs, which numbered about forty:

They'd been shut in for days, and their squealing nearly drove us mad. In the end I persuaded a pal to come with me, and we dodged the bullets and let them out.

I shan't forget the sight of those pigs in a hurry. They were so thin they looked like kangaroos, and when we opened the gate they swarmed over us and bolted. They were more trouble out than in. They got everywhere, more like wild animals than the tame kind we know.

Henry recounted a story of the Scots Fusiliers who thought they heard someone tampering with the barbed wire in front of their position and so, quite understandably, opened fire. When daylight came they discovered that they had killed a pig.

The second day of fighting saw the Germans move a field gun onto the ridge in front of the Green Howards. Henry and the others had improvised some shelter using doors, shelves and shutters from the buildings around them. The Germans though were intent on shelling the buildings, some of which contained dressing stations and still had some wounded soldiers in them. Henry takes up the story:

> Squirming out of our trenches, we started to crawl forward. There was no cover to speak of; you had to take a chance whether they got you. As it happened we were lucky. We managed to get all the wounded back without a casualty!

In 1923 the Green Howards commissioned a painting, which would subsequently be hung in the officers' mess, based on a sketch by an artist named Fortunino Matania. The painting depicts the evacuation of the wounded that Henry describes above, at Petit Kruiseke, which is near the Menin Crossroads, and shows in the right foreground the figure of Henry carrying a wounded soldier on his back. By 1923, Henry was close to leaving the army and was, in any event, with the Duke of Wellington's Regiment, so it is quite probable that he knew nothing of the painting or the part it would play in his later life.

For Henry the action was not quite over and he remembered a further incident:

> And once in the night a torch flashed on and I saw a German calmly cutting our wire. I knocked him down and crawled out and brought him in. He said he hadn't realised we were so close. Trench warfare was young in those days you must remember.

It had been a costly action for the Green Howards and when the battalion was finally relieved on 29 October and a roll call taken, it revealed that of the original 1,000 men, only 300 answered to their names. This was a dark time for Henry and the other survivors as they stood there listening to the names of individuals they knew being called out and going unanswered. The battle itself did not end until 22 November.

The First Battle of Ypres was the last open warfare battle before the Western Front became some 450 miles of virtually static trenches, barbed wire, sniping, patrols, mud, carnage and a place of extreme discomfort for the soldiers.

For Henry and his regular army comrades this would have been their introduction to a new form of warfare, where new, 'industrial' forms of weaponry were deployed in the form of machine guns and heavy artillery. It was also to be a war where the soldiers from both armies were to face each other from their respective trenches as they looked across no-man's-land.

★★★

Looked at from the air, the British trench system was three parallel lines namely the front, support and reserve trenches. The front line would have been somewhat zigzagged in nature to prevent enfilade fire and to give some protection from shell blasts. Spaced along it would have been trench bays, which Brown (2000) says would have been some 18ft to 30ft in length and occupied by a small group of soldiers. Henry would have found himself in such a group and these men would have become his main circle of acquaintances, although this would have been a group with an ever-changing membership reflecting those killed, wounded, sick or on leave. This group would have been Henry's 'mates', but over time he would have learnt not to get too attached to individuals who might well be there one day but not the next.

Going up the line was preceded by the soldiers being issued with a supply of tinned corned beef, known as bully beef, biscuits and ammunition, and them being ordered to destroy all personal papers. Although the official reason for this was to ensure that if shot or wounded, a soldier's documents would not supply the enemy with useful intelligence, it would have also sent a very clear message to the men about the reality of war and their own mortality.

In what time was available, the soldiers would write hurried letters home to their loved ones, and it is sad that no letters from Henry have survived. It is, of course, quite possible that Henry may not have sent any letters at all, because there is no evidence that he enjoyed anything approaching a close relationship with any members of his family. He was known to be a quiet man and so perhaps he preferred not to worry his family, or risk the censor's pen, and made do with sending them a Field Service postcard instead.

Henry's life in the trenches would have settled into a steady routine commencing with stand-to in the hour before dawn. Standing-to, on the trench's fire step along with his comrades, Henry would have looked out across no-man's-land in case the enemy sprung a surprise attack whilst visibility was reduced, but once the enemy lines could be clearly seen then all those apart from sentries would be stood down. Stand down saw each man issued with a tot of rum which had to be drunk in the presence of an officer.

Breakfast would consist of rations that had been brought up the lines the night before by fatigue parties, and if Henry was lucky this would be tea, bread and bacon, otherwise it would be bully beef and biscuits. According to Holmes (2005), a soldier's bully beef and biscuits could only be eaten if no other food was available, and to do otherwise was treated as an offence, but it was not unknown for fatigue parties bringing up rations to suffer casualties or indeed be wiped out. There would also be tins of pork and beans, maconochie (vegetables and meat) and jam. When possible, the men would also receive fresh food supplies of meat, bacon and vegetables, which may have been uncooked or partially cooked. In the case of partially cooked food the men would finish the cooking themselves. Holmes tells how the soldiers would use 'tommy cookers', described as 'a small tin holding a chunk of solid fuel or a pot of meths on which a mess tin full of water or tinned food was heated'.

Army rations would also be supplemented by what could be purchased from the locals, who became the target of complaints from the soldiers about over pricing, and by food parcels sent from home. Henry and his comrades from the trench bay would have pooled their resources, and it was not uncommon for parcels addressed to soldiers who had been killed to be opened and shared out. Food parcels were distributed when the soldiers were out of the line and anything that did not require eating straight away was put into their haversacks to be eaten when they went back up the line.

Both the tea and the water would come up the line in old petrol tins, which had an inevitable effect on the taste of the contents.

After breakfast, Henry and his comrades would have their rifles inspected, which involved checking that no part was adversely affected by mud or other dirt. If Henry was not on sentry duty then he would set to on a variety of duties that, with breaks for lunch and an evening meal, would take him through to about 6 p.m.

There would be another stand-to at dusk, followed by a further inspection. Holmes states that:

> The British Army marched less on its stomach than in a haze of smoke. Woodbines hung from pale lips, black cutty pipes jutted fiercely from beneath Old Bill moustaches, and Virginia cigarettes dangled from well manicured fingers.

So, whatever the soldiers were doing, the majority would have been smoking either cigarettes or a pipe, and although there is no evidence either way, the likelihood is that Henry would have been a smoker. (If Henry was a smoker at this time, he certainly did not smoke in later life.) Remarkably, when looked at from today's knowledge of the link between smoking and cancer, cigarettes and tobacco were issued free to the men, just as any other ration. They were also sent in parcels from home, and could be bought in canteens or from shops when out of the line. Inevitably they were also used to trade for goods or services that were not routinely available, such as a haircut.

As with smoking, it is reasonable to assume that Henry would have drunk alcohol and although it was not freely available he would have received a daily rum allowance of 1/16 pint, which, as previously mentioned, was only issued under supervision. The issuing of the rum ration was supervised to avoid any abuse leading to drunkenness, although this does seem to have occurred on occasions. A drunken soldier in the trenches would have been a liability and a danger to those around him, through their noise, aggression or a simple inability to carry out orders. When out of the line there were opportunities to buy wine or beer either from canteens or local bars; however, NCOs and men were not allowed to drink spirits.

Toilet facilities, known as latrines, were not, unexpectedly, that primitive; the army still expected these to be kept in good order, with each company having a sanitary corporal for this purpose. They were periodically the subject of inspection by officers together with medical staff, and in 1917 a Major G.O. Chambers, attached to the medical staff of the Cavalry Corps, gave the following report on the latrines of the 1st Life Guards (Holmes):

> Latrines. Fly proof pails – sufficient in quantity. Urine tubs being in front of latrines in recess of trench – ground soiled with urine.

He recommended that they should be moved and a splash board installed 'to prevent dripping'.

A latrine would either consist of a bucket or what was known as a 'deep drop' which was topped by a pole. Buckets would be emptied into nearby shell holes and covered with earth and chloride of lime. The deep-drop latrines had soil thrown down to cover the human waste.

The latrines were certainly not havens of peace and tranquillity as from time to time those using them would be killed or wounded by enemy fire.

★★★

As has been already stated, there are no surviving letters or diaries where Henry is concerned, but if there were, it would be no surprise to read his complaints about having to endure long marches in boots that were unsuitable for marching on cobbled or other hard road surfaces. Brown (2001) makes the point that although weaponry was developed and produced on an increasingly large scale, little thought was given to improving the mobility of the troops. One image from the Great War is that of the use of London buses to move soldiers from one place to another. It did happen and it made for good public relations news footage, but it accounted for a small proportion of the transport needs which generally was met by the soldiers marching.

A description of typical marching conditions is given by Lance Corporal R. Mountfort of the 10th Battalion of the Royal Fusiliers:

> We marched fifteen miles on Wednesday. It doesn't sound much but when you think of the heat of the day, the weight of the packs, and the state of the French roads you will understand it was an amazing strain on our endurance. The French roads are horrible. Through every village and for a mile or two each side they are composed of great rough cobblestones, about eight inches square and not overly carefully laid. Apart from the unevenness there is the difficulty that the nails of our boots step on them as on ice.

The conditions facing the men included dust, thirst, heat and the variable road surface, depending on the time of year. Soldiers would have found little to drink as they marched, as drinking from their water bottles was treated as an offence and would be punished. It is unsurprising, therefore, that there were occasions when men died whilst marching.

★★★

Like any soldier in the trenches, Henry would have to take his turn on sentry duty both during the day and at night, generally for no more than one hour at a time. The Germans did not stay passively in their trenches at night, and so the sentries had to remain alert and vigilant. The importance of the sentry role is underlined by the fact that to be caught asleep on such duty was viewed as a capital offence because it could ultimately endanger the whole military unit. Many more soldiers fell asleep on sentry duty than were ever caught, and if caught the lucky ones would just receive a reprimand.

The troops would find themselves spending on average five days in the front line, five days in reserve, five days in the front line and finally five days in reserve, which was then followed by being relieved and returning to the rear.

Once darkness fell, those soldiers not on sentry duty would be involved in a variety of activities that needed to be undertaken in darkness, such as trench repairs, wire repair or wire-cutting parties, and patrols. These were still dangerous activities as the enemy might still fire a pre-aimed machine gun across the British trench parapet, or send up flares that could reveal a party of soldiers in no-man's-land.

Inevitably, Henry would have found himself detailed to take part in patrols and these would have been for either reconnaissance or fighting purposes. A reconnaissance patrol was about obtaining information and returning with it either in the form of captured documents or individuals, or the effective identification of the regiments which were holding the line opposite. A fighting patrol, which later became known as a raid, was, as Brown (2000) describes:

> A small but murderous attack against enemy trenches, which were occupied briefly by raiders, who inflicted in minutes the maximum of death and destruction upon the enemy, and then got out before he counter-attacked.

The raids would have taken place at night across no-man's-land. Care would have been taken to conceal their presence; their skin would have been darkened to avoid being seen, their equipment secured to avoid rattling noises, and the advancing men would freeze like statues in the event that an enemy flare lit up the night sky. On arrival at the enemy lines it would be necessary for the barbed wire to be checked for gaps and if none existed then it had to be cut. The attack on the enemy trench would involve throwing bombs, the use of the bayonet, clubs and small arms fire. Some men became specialists in the various elements of the trench raid and were, as a result, spared from other duties.

Lieutenant Wyatt wrote in his diary on 6 February 1915 about a patrol showing that, despite the horrors of war, soldiers could still display some humour:

Went out and crawled very bravely close to the German barbed wire. They stayed a long time and listened and they were just about to crawl back when a voice from the German trenches said in perfect English, 'if you don't go away soon we shall really have to shoot you.' They went.

Sometimes when a raid was to take place volunteers would be asked for and although there is no evidence for it, it is possible that, given his subsequent bravery, Henry would have put himself forward. For someone who had joined the army to be a soldier, and therefore to fight, taking part in a raid would have been far more exciting than simply existing in a trench waiting for something to happen and being reactive. It would have provided an opportunity to do something and be proactive. Of course, the British Army did not have exclusive rights to trench raids and so Henry may have seen or experienced German raids and had to deal with their aftermath.

Henry and the other men would have been at constant risk of being shot by a sniper. Sniping was seen as 'a means both of causing loss to the enemy and of controlling overt forms of live and let live' (Ashworth, 2000). The soldiers themselves would have favoured a quiet life, so if the Germans did not fire at them then why should they fire back? However, their officers, particularly headquarters staff, saw things differently and knew that if the Germans were harassed they would respond, keeping their own men alert and involved.

Brown quotes an Australian soldier as saying that 'none save the very rash would dare to thrust his head over the top, for the snipers on both sides were appallingly quick and accurate'. Sniping also had an adverse effect on the morale of the enemy. It is hard to imagine the effect of seeing a comrade killed in this way, by a solitary bullet through the head. Holmes (2005) describes the experience of one Henry Williamson:

Crack! And the man next to you stared at you curiously for a moment. Then you saw a hole in his forehead and when he slid down you saw that the back of his head was open.

One minute they would have been going about their daily life in the trench and then, as the result of a second's thoughtlessness or distraction causing them to raise their head higher than they should, their life would be extinguished.

Henry would have learnt to adapt to this very real threat by keeping his head down at all times and avoiding, if possible, exposed parts of the trench system. When a machine-gunner or an artilleryman fires their weapon, even if they can see their enemy, it is not personalised in the sense that they select a specific soldier to shoot and in doing so ignore others in making their choice. This is the reason why enemy snipers were so reviled and rarely spared, as can be sensed in the following diary entry from a Captain Patterson (Brown, 2001) on 24 September:

> If I am to be killed let it be in the heat and rush of an advance and not by a dirty sniper who waits his chance for perhaps hours.

The machine gun was an out-and-out killing machine capable of firing hundreds of rounds a minute over distances of up to 2,500 yards to devastating effect on advancing soldiers. There are many descriptions of lines of men being mown down like a row of young saplings, and it is one of the enduring images of the Great War of men going over the top and marching stoically across no-man's-land only to be cut down by the enemy machine guns. However, equally deadly was the machine gun that had been set up to sweep across the top of a trench parapet, or direct its fire at a deliberately placed and tempting gap in the wire.

Artillery with its high-explosive shells and shrapnel could destroy barbed wire and trench systems as a prelude to an attack. Henry would have experienced cowering helplessly in the trenches as the enemy bombarded the lines, as well as advancing through enemy artillery fire, seeing comrades cut down by shrapnel or effectively vaporised as a shell exploded. It was also the case that the blast alone could cause death by concussion, leaving no surface marks on the body.

Winter (1979) talks of the differing uses for the artillery, starting with 'the least feared were those shells that came over in bunches on the hour just to warn that the enemy was on his toes', moving to 'isolated shots' aimed at a particular target, and finishing with the pre-attack barrages. He describes the effect of the barrage as 'like a dentist's drill on a sensitive tooth without anaesthetic'. For those on the receiving end it was a real test of nerves that literally drove some men mad. Sadly, there were also instances of Allied artillery inadvertently shelling their own men, either because shells fell short of their target, or because when a trench was successfully taken the artillery believed that it was still held by the Germans.

As the war progressed, Henry would have become aware of the increasing danger from the air as the role and arms of the enemy air forces developed. In the early years it would be a case of the enemy pilot swooping low over men and trenches and firing his revolver, or dropping the hideous darts that can now be seen in many museums. Over time enemy planes would drop bombs and strafe men and trenches with machine guns. The men did not really have any defences against air attack, other than taking cover, but occasionally an enemy plane would be brought down by rifle fire.

By 1916, those in the front line had to face up to the use of flame-throwers, which sent burning oil as a jet, some 6ft across, up to 25 yards from a hand-held nozzle coming from a container strapped to a man's back. This fearsome weapon produced noise, black clouds of smoke, and terror. As the container had to be of a size that could be carried on a man's back the liquid soon ran out, although quite often this process would be hastened by its operator being shot down.

It is impossible to read about life in the trenches without being aware of the issue of lice, caused by so many men being in such close proximity to each other. The occasions when the troops were taken out of the line provided opportunities for bathing, a change of clothing and delousing. Brown (2001) comments on another sound effect heard on the front:

Along with the crump of shells and the sputter of rifle or machine gun fire, was the cracking noise resulting from the running of lighted cigarettes or matches along the seams of shirts and trousers, the trench louse's favourite habitation.

Henry may also have resorted to another much-used method of lice control, involving running his fingernail through the seams of his clothing. The lice were referred to as 'chats' and their removal became known as 'chatting' – the men would sit together 'chatting'. How many people today, when they chat to friends and family, know that what they are doing was derived from the term for removing lice?

Groom (2003) talks of the despair experienced by soldiers on discovering that they were lousy and the resulting effect on morale. This is surely how Henry would have felt, and on top of the fear and torment of the German soldiers and the equipment they had at their disposal, here was a creature that epitomised dirt and grubbiness to torment him further. The lice would turn black as they gorged on their host's blood, and this could result in soldiers going down with trench fever necessitating time out of the line, with some, in fact, never returning.

Another nuisance for Henry, on finding himself in the trenches, would have been the rats, because, as Groom says:

> They feasted on corpses and carcasses in the trenches and in no-man's-land until some said they were as big as cats, and twice as bold. Men shot them, bayoneted them, poisoned them, and beat them with clubs but in the long run to no avail.

Initially, taking on the rats would have represented some light relief or sport, but over time, particularly as they became associated with death and feeding on the bodies of not just the dead but at times the wounded, they would have become another ever-present horror to the soldiers. The rats seemed to know no fear and would walk across sleeping men, on occasions biting them and eating their rations and candles, which for many were a key source of light.

The winter of 1914–15 would also have been Henry's first experience of the bitter cold and wet of Flanders. Clothing would become wet through, almost impossible to dry and covered in mud. The weather would be bitterly cold with strong winds, rain and snow. Brown quotes from a letter sent by Robert Mcfie, a colour quartermaster sergeant of the Territorial Battalion, the 10th King's Liverpool Regiment, parts of which bring this winter vividly to life:

> We went into the trenches cold and wet for there was heavy rain and a snowstorm … When we came out we were colder, wetter and ever so much muddier. The next morning I found that all the exposed parts of my skin were thickly coated with hard mud (my clothes of course were worse) … We wear anything we like. We are not in the least like a regiment in England, spotlessly clean, all dressed precisely alike, and every man erect, and every button in place. We have woollen headgear, comforters that wave in the wind, gloves of various colours … Our legs are covered indifferently by spats, puttees, or hose tops from home.

Henry would have been issued with a great coat which would have been heavy, cumbersome and would have absorbed the wet that was all around. He almost certainly, along with many of the other soldiers, would have preferred to wear one of the sleeveless jackets made from goatskins that were issued in late 1914, switching to a hard-wearing leather version in 1915.

Trenches were invariably full of water, necessitating, where possible, attempts at pumping this out with varying degrees of success. Soldiers could find themselves standing knee-deep or worse in water or mud and the cold would seep into their bones. It was a constant struggle to even attempt to keep things dry and was yet something else to contend with which sapped morale.

The pay for a private soldier was 1s a day, for which no conditions of service were attached other than to do as the army told them. To do otherwise constituted a punishable offence.

★★★

It must be assumed that during the course of the war Henry would have enjoyed periods of leave, although these were unpredictable in terms of timing and length. Some men served long periods of time without enjoying a spell of leave. Today, this seems unfair, but in its defence the army was dealing with millions of men and lacked the necessary administration until 1916 when lists were kept and rotas determined who went on leave.

The period of leave also included travelling time, which, although an issue for all soldiers, was a particular issue for those living long distances away from the south-east of England. Those soldiers would spend the bulk of their leave travelling and consequently very little time with their family and friends.

★★★

A significant antidote to what the soldiers had to face was humour. Brown quotes from a letter written by Captain Eric Gore-Brown in 1915:

> One has to be absolutely all there all the time and hang on to one's humour like grim death – otherwise I think you are bound to crack.

The soldiers' humour would have been oral, quite often dark and almost certainly not for polite society, but there were also service magazines and newspapers such as the famous *Wipers Times*. These publications were full of in-jokes, with the colour of the humour somewhat toned down. Even today the *Wipers Times* is a fascinating and humorous read.

Humour proved essential to help the soldiers live and work, and for the maintenance of their morale generally, but even so as the war dragged on its effect may well have diminished over time.

★★★

Henry may have been aware of cases of cowardice and desertion, although these were somewhat rare between August 1914 and the end of that year. According to Babington (1986) there were three cases of desertion and one of cowardice, which resulted in the offenders' execution on the Western Front. The numbers grew in 1915 with fifty-one soldiers executed for desertion (forty-five), cowardice (three), quitting their post (one) and murder (two).

During the war it was the practice, although there was no firm rule about this, to have men from the condemned man's own unit form the firing squad, and in most cases to determine the place of execution. Sometimes the division or brigade headquarters would intervene and select the site of the execution. Did deterrence work? Babington states that in 1916 there were ninety-six executions on the Western Front, ninety-four in 1917 and forty-four in 1918. But the executions did not stop with the end of the war as a further nine were carried out in 1919 and two in 1920.

Executions were generally carried out at daybreak, and sometimes in the presence of men from the condemned soldier's battalion or platoon. In performing an execution the army was looking to punish the individual concerned, but also to deter others from committing the same offence, and deterrence in the view of some commanding officers necessitated an audience. And why should there be any surprise that in cases with the clearest mitigating evidence the army commanders still persisted with the death penalty, as, after all, were they not condemning their men to death every time they ordered an advance or a trench raid?

The firing squad would normally be made up of one officer and ten men. In his book, Babington describes the rituals surrounding an execution with the officer loading the rifles of the firing squad, putting live ammunition in nine and a blank in the other. Babington says that:

Right up to the moment of taking aim, each member of the firing party could continue to hope that he alone might be absolved from playing a part in the killing of a comrade.

The officer carried a revolver and would give the order to fire and, in the event of the condemned man surviving the volley, would have to approach him and complete the execution. If the members of the firing squad hoped that their bullet was the blank, then what must the officer have been thinking?

Soldiers who had been executed were later buried in the same cemeteries as their comrades who had died in action. In September 1916, the adjutant general issued an order which read:

> There is no rule that any man who has suffered the extreme penalty of the law should be buried near the place of execution. Any man who suffers the extreme penalty of the law may be buried in a cemetery, the inscription being marked DIED instead of KILLED IN ACTION or DIED OF WOUNDS.

In the case of the 2nd Battalion, Drummer Rose, who in all probability would have been known to Henry, deserted in December 1914 and remained absent until December 1916. Following his capture a contrite Rose cited family and personal issues at his court martial as the reasons for his desertion, but the court was unimpressed and found him guilty, sentencing him to death. He was executed by firing squad on 4 March 1917, by which time Henry was hospitalised in Britain for treatment of a wound received at the Somme and, therefore, he would not have witnessed or been a member of the firing squad.

★★★

This was suddenly the war that Henry found himself in and although he did not know it at the time, these were the conditions in which he would have to exist for most of the coming four years. How would Henry have felt as the war started to drag on from one year to the next? Henry and the others would have entered the war in a state of unconscious ignorance – they did not know what they did not know – but as the war progressed that would have quickly changed. Having experienced one winter in the trenches, how did they feel when it became apparent that that experience was to be repeated? It is truly unimaginable.

In today's age of instant and all-day news channels, embedded reporters, Facebook, Twitter and mobile phones with cameras the public has now become familiar with images from the battlefield being available almost instantly. The repatriation of the dead and their subsequent funerals has become an all too familiar sight. Almost the instant that a soldier has been killed in action details are carried on the news channels, but it was not like that in the First World War.

Filmed images of the war were limited and many of the scenes depicted were staged for the cameras. The authorities, due to the limited number of news outlets, were able to control the news, and this, together with the inevitable delays in relaying stories back to Britain, meant that the public had a distorted view of events, and were to some extent shielded from the full picture and horrors of the Western Front. Today, it is easy to imagine the way the general public would react to a news story about several thousand soldiers having been killed or wounded in one day, or scenes of scores of coffins being carried down the ramp of a transport plane. There would be an overwhelming loss of support for continuing such a war, and pressure on the government of the day to bring the troops home.

Where Henry is concerned the lack of a surviving diary or letters to family is compounded by his apparent reluctance to talk about his experiences on the Western Front in his later life, as none of the relatives spoken to while researching this book can recall any stories being passed down through the family. It means that what he saw and what he thought will sadly never be known. This reluctance to speak to family and friends was not uncommon among veterans who kept their experiences bottled up. Reunions provided some opportunity to talk more openly with other veterans, but even then the tendency was to speak of the positive experiences.

★★★

The importance of the First Battle of Ypres, which lasted from 19 October to 22 November 1914, was that it stopped the Germans from capturing the Channel ports and thereby threatening both Britain and France, but it came at a high cost with more than 56,000 casualties. The men of the BEF were irreplaceable because they were regular soldiers and therefore trained troops. In due course their places would be taken by the Territorial Force (formed in 1908 and largely furnished with outdated equipment), Kitchener's volunteer (or new) armies which had been in training since August and entered the field in 1915, and then from 1916 conscription was introduced.

It is not known whether Henry participated in the Christmas Truce of 1914, but that Christmas and New Year period saw his battalion in receipt of an unusual message from the Germans, as recorded in Lieutenant Wyatt's diary entry for 30 December:

> Same routine as before. Still no war. At about lunchtime however a message came down the line to say that Germans had sent across to say that their own general was coming along in the afternoon, so we had better keep down as they might have to do a little shooting to make things look right!!! And this is war!! This we did, and a few shots came over about 3.30pm.

The division suffered so many casualties that it did not return to full fighting strength until early 1915.

HITLER IN 1914

Although there is a considerable amount of literature available where Hitler's war service is concerned, it is important to bear in mind that there are possibly two versions. One version was written contemporaneously when Hitler was an unknown soldier, and the later versions were written just before and after he came to power. In the latter case this was written either by those seeking to ingratiate themselves with Hitler, or in furtherance of propaganda and the building of his self-mythology. Where possible these differences will be pointed out.

Despite the apparent discrepancies between the two versions of Hitler's war service it must be borne in mind that he served on the Western Front from 1914 until 1918, and therefore it is fair to consider him as brave as anyone else who served there. Those serving with him had no idea who or what he would become in later years, and undoubtedly he was wounded and did receive gallantry awards. This book does not seek to undermine his record as a soldier in the Great War, but is interested in the way that Hitler and the Nazi propaganda machine stretched and overstated his service, experience and actions.

Hitler did not want to serve in the Austrian Army and had been evading the authorities since 1910, but in early 1914 he was found in Munich. He was given the choice of reporting to the Austrian Consulate or face extradition. Whether it was as a result of his lifestyle or a deliberate attempt to fool the Austrian military service, at his screening on 15 February 1914 he would not have been disappointed to be told that he was deemed too weak to bear arms – unsurprising since his appearance was described by Williams (2005) as emaciated and malnourished.

It was the First World War that gave Hitler his life direction and a cause to which he could commit himself totally. On 2 August 1914, Hitler was in the crowd that gathered in the Odeonplatz, Munich, to hear the proclamation of German mobilisation (Keegan, 1998). He wrote later that he was 'carried away by the enthusiasm of the moment and I sank down upon my knees and thanked Heaven out of the fullness of my heart for the favour of having been permitted to live in such a time' (Verhey, 2000). As Kershaw (1998) says, 'The First World War made Hitler possible'.

On 5 August, Hitler, now determined to enlist in the German Army despite his Austrian citizenship, petitioned the court of King Ludwig III of Bavaria for permission to serve in the King's Own Regiment but without success. Instead, on 16 August he volunteered for the 16th Bavarian Reserve Infantry Regiment, also known as the List Regiment after its commanding officer. Initial training took place in Munich, followed by exercises at Lechfeld, near Augsburg. During this period, on 8 October, Hitler swore his oath to serve King Ludwig III.

On 20 October the regiment entrained for the front, and after a two-day journey it arrived in Lille and was promptly attached to the 6th Bavarian Division in Crown Prince Rupprecht's Sixth Army, but, according to Weber (2010), the regiment was as ill-disciplined as it had been in its early days at Lechfeld, and few knew how to use the Gewehr 98 standard German battle rifle properly.

Williams states that initially the regiment was granted three days' leave, with Hitler spending the night of the 27th in a dugout with a decomposing horse, before moving to a farmhouse for the following night. The conditions experienced by the Germans would have been no different to those on the British side, so Henry and Hitler had much in common in terms of experience.

The German army was in the throes of fighting the First Battle of Ypres and Hitler's regiment saw its first action on 29 October some 5 miles east of Ypres on the Menin Road (Kershaw), but were driven back by the British resulting in serious casualties. The regiment was to take part in the German assault of Gheluvelt and the drive to take Ypres, although this was in less than ideal conditions, as there was heavy fog restricting visibility to less than 130ft (Weber). As the Germans crossed the British trenches their indiscipline led to them not checking that the trenches had been cleared. Consequently the British were able shoot them from both the front and the rear.

The regiment and Hitler, described by Weber as 'a simple infantryman', charged the enemy and engaged in hand-to-hand fighting, sustaining heavy casualties.

Action on the 30th also saw further severe losses sustained in rainy and cold conditions. The Germans managed to take Gheluvelt but could not hold the village. Hitler and others of the List Regiment found themselves in the comparative comfort of a British trench outside the village's castle.

On 1 November the regiment was withdrawn from the line, and on the 8th they took over a line of trenches at Messines; it was at this point that Hitler was assigned to the regimental headquarters as one of a group of six to ten despatch runners. Their task was to carry orders on foot, or sometimes by bicycle, from the regimental command post to the battalion and company commanders at the front some 2 miles away.

The Germans had failed to make the breakthrough they desperately wanted but this did not stop Hitler writing to friends in Munich and claiming a victory (Weber), knowing that the enemy regiment had been reduced from 3,000 men and twenty-five officers to 725 men and four officers.

Also at this time he was promoted to *Gefreiter*, a rank that was some way short of corporal, by which Hitler is wrongly referred to, particularly as it did not give him authority over others (Weber). This was to be his last promotion of the war, although 'given his length of service, and service at Regimental Headquarters, he could have been expected to advance further to at least the rank of a non-commissioned officer'.

He was later nominated for promotion, even though his superiors thought him lacking in leadership (Kershaw), but Hitler himself did not want promotion as this would have resulted in his being reassigned from his messenger group, which he thought of as his family (Williams). On 9 November, Hitler was made a despatch runner and assigned to regimental headquarters.

From 15–17 November, the regiment was involved in fighting at Wytschaete, and it was here that Hitler earned an Iron Cross Second Class:

> During the fighting Hitler's commanding officer was wounded and lay in the open near a burning church. Exposing himself to dangerous fire Hitler crawled out to rescue him. (Groom, 2003)

According to a report in 1915 (Weber), there were four despatch runners involved and the hero was really one of them, a man by the name of Bachmann, rather than Hitler. Weber suggests that the version placing Hitler as the hero is based on a 1932 report written the year before Hitler came to power, which is different to the 1915 report written when he was unknown. It is not difficult to work out why that might have been the case!

Irrespective of this discrepancy, the fact is that Hitler did receive his Iron Cross on 2 December. But as will be seen later, where Henry is concerned the Germans were no more consistent or fair in the distribution of bravery awards than the British. Weber says that awards were more likely to go to those soldiers who were known to the officers of the regimental headquarters, and therefore Hitler's award cannot necessarily be taken as a demonstration that he was braver than those around him.

It was also during the fighting on 17 November that Hitler escaped death or injury, having left a forward command post just before it was struck by a shell, which left those still there either dead or wounded (Kershaw). On 20 November the regiment was moved back into the divisional reserve and then back to the front line on 26 December.

Williams said that by the end of 1914 Hitler 'had the reputation of being not only capable but strange: a man who lives in his own world'. Hitler had survived the first months of the war but it is open to debate as to whether this was because he was capable or just lucky, given that Weber sees him as a weak young man with little military training.

★★★

Adolf Hitler and the List Regiment arrived at Ypres nearly two weeks or so after Henry, and joined the First Battle of Ypres a week after it started. On this occasion they were certainly in reasonably close proximity, even if totally unaware of each other and how their stories would unfold.

Both men would have shared — albeit in Hitler's case for a short time — similar experiences of life in the trenches. Lice and rats did not care about such things as nationality; mud was mud; the weather affected both equally; and the means of death remained the same for both.

However, there was one significant difference between them: there is no record of the war turning Henry towards politics unlike Hitler, who even at this stage was starting to develop the ideas which would eventually result in him becoming the German Führer and architect of the Second World War.

1915

The year opened with fresh hope and with the 2nd Battalion in reserve, supposedly for rest and recuperation (R&R). This would have represented a welcome respite from the dangers and unpleasant conditions of the trenches, although there was still the risk of enemy shells and attacks from enemy aircraft. But quite often R&R actually meant the opposite, as detailed by Lieutenant Bernard White of the 20th Battalion, Northumberland Fusiliers (Gilbert, 2007):

> There are kit inspections, anti-gas helmet inspections, ration inspections, rifle inspections, foot inspections, route marches, bathing parades, laundry parades, and working parties.

However, Henry would have appreciated much of what R&R entailed, particularly the chance to have a bath and a change of clothing, to get some unbroken sleep and to enjoy better food.

It is hard to imagine that Henry and the other soldiers enjoyed being dirty and inevitably a bit smelly. Those men coming from the front looked like tramps as they were unshaven and covered in mud, and they would have rejoiced at the opportunity to take a bath in whatever was available, from beer barrels to laundry tubs. Winter describes the process:

> Parties of fifty would be marched in, in alphabetical order. They would leave outside their underclothes to be soaked for four hours in creosol, and their uniforms wrapped in their identity discs and handled by nubile young refugee girls from Belgium. The vigorous nudity of an

unending cavalcade of young men gave great and noisy pleasure to both sides. A cold hosepipe would serve the dual purpose of driving out the men and washing off the suds ready for the fresh uniforms, theoretically de-loused.

The baths could be operating for twelve hours a day, processing up to a thousand men in that time.

To add to the excitement the boilers may not have worked, resulting in cold water, or alternatively the water might have run out. Winter says that the issue of clean clothing was a lottery, with the men invariably receiving underwear or socks in the wrong size, or clean shirts with soiled underwear. Unless the clothing issued was brand new then it would come with lice already present, which would become active with the warmth of a man's body.

Inevitably, Henry and the others would have wondered how rest equated with working parties, which could mean moving stores and equipment up to the front and other physical labour. This far from restful rest unsurprisingly led to complaints, a point made in Lieutenant Wyatt's diary entry for 12 January (Brown, 2001):

On fatigue for the RE. I think it is shameful the way men are put on fatigues when out of the trenches. Rest! A lot of rest they get! It doesn't give them a chance to get dry even. However such is war.

Away from the fatigues, the men had the opportunity to spend their pay, which soldiers starting their R&R would have received in local currency on the first morning, in a variety of ways. Tobacco, food and weak beer were the obvious purchases, and no period behind the line was complete without time spent at a local *estaminet*, where local wine, coffee, and egg and chips could be enjoyed at a price, or bought from local people.

The army also encouraged the men to join in on sports days, form their own concert parties to put on shows or to attend shows performed by professionals, which would be a mix of popular songs and sketches. The men also enjoyed gambling either to increase the amount of money in their pockets or to replace what they had spent. The army frowned on gambling because of the possible effect on morale, and went no further than officially sanctioned bingo.

Once the men were rested, bathed with a change of clothes, fed, paid and taken a drink, the last thing on their minds was a game of bingo, and so many would have sought out the company of women. Brothels were common in the rest areas and were sanctioned by the army to the extent that there were separate establishments for officers and men.

There is, of course, no evidence that Henry visited these places but if he did then he needed to be mindful of two things. Firstly, to make sure he visited the correct establishment as indicated by the colour of the lamp hanging outside, namely red for the men and blue for the officers (Winter), and, secondly, to ensure that he did not contract a venereal disease.

Winter says in his book that venereal disease accounted for 27 per cent of hospitalisations. Even though the army took a necessarily serious view of the contraction of a venereal disease, as those affected would be out of the line for a number of weeks while being treated, they struggled to tackle it. An enlightened approach would have been to accept that the men would visit brothels and issue them with contraceptives, as well as ensuring that the prostitutes themselves were disease free through regulation and inspection. The army chose not to do that and instead instituted random inspections, where the men would stand in line with their trousers and underwear pulled down in preparation for their genitals to be inspected by, usually, a young and inexperienced officer. Those found to be infected were considered to be sick through negligence and were punished by pay deductions and loss of leave. It is likely that the army felt the inspections would be so embarrassing for the men that the problem would go away, but men continued to act as men, and it is all too easy to believe that the rounds provided yet another opportunity for humour, probably at the expense of the young officer. As such, whether or not Henry was a frequenter of brothels he would still have experienced these periodic, random inspections.

If the men were running short of money or were looking for something quieter, then the YMCA provided an opportunity for the men to get together to drink tea, eat sandwiches or generally kill time. The YMCA also provided paper for the men to write letters home. Letter writing was generally a problematic area for soldiers. If they wrote what they really wanted to talk about they knew that their letters would be subjected to censorship and the obliterating pen of an officer. Because of censorship or an unwillingness to worry loved ones at home, some soldiers resorted to little more than platitudes, or used the Field Service postcards provided by the army, where all that was required was for the appropriate boxes to be ticked or deleted, along the lines of:

> I am quite well.
> I have been admitted into hospital – sick/wounded – am getting on well/hope to be discharged soon.
> I have received your letter/telegram/parcel.
> Letter follows at first opportunity.

As has been stated earlier, if Henry sent letters home from the front then none have survived.

★★★

Conditions in the winter of 1914–15 would have been a very new experience for Henry and his comrades, and this is captured by a further entry in Lieutenant Wyatt's diary, dated 17 February:

> Miserably cold and wet. The way the men stand the weather is marvellous, with no spells in fairly comfortable billets to help them, and far less leave in England to refresh them, except for the very few.

For Henry, 1915 saw the 7th Division involved in the battles of Neuve Chappelle, Aubers, Festubert, Givenchy and Loos, which Keegan (1983) described as a 'series of minor, murderous, trench to trench battles' characterised 'by the extreme ferocity of the fighting and the miserable physical conditions'.

★★★

The year 1915 also saw the first use of gas attacks by the Germans. Tear gas had been used in January, but in April the Germans progressed from using gas to disable the enemy to using it as a means of killing, with the introduction of chlorine, followed by phosgene in December and mustard gas in July 1917.

Chlorine gas turned out to be an avoidable killer largely because it smelt and could be seen, thereby giving those under attack time to take preventative action, which could be as little as clamping a handkerchief over the nose and mouth. It was still a killer though because if breathed in sufficient quantities it would destroy the lungs and bronchial tubes, leaving those affected drowning in the liquid that the gas caused to fill up their lungs.

Phosgene was a much stronger gas which could not be seen but carried an odour that was described as being like mouldy hay. An individual could have been subjected to a fatal dose before they were aware of the smell's true nature. Again, the gas attacked the lungs, producing 'four pints of yellow liquid from the lungs each hour for the forty eight hours of the drowning spasm' (Winter, 1979).

Mustard gas was about causing a disturbance among the enemy as much as killing. With this gas the effects only became apparent three hours after exposure, which Winter describes as:

> Sneezing and copious mucus would develop as if a dose of flu was on the way. Then the eyelids would swell and close with an accompanying sensation of burning in the throat. Where bare skin had been exposed, moist red patches just as in scarlet fever grew, the patches becoming massive blisters within twenty four hours. Thereafter there would arrive severe headaches, rise in pulse rate and temperature, pneumonia ... In more severe exposures men might cough up a cast of their mucous membranes, lose their genitals, or be burnt through to the bone.

The initial defence against gas attack would have involved field dressings soaked in alkaline bicarbonate of soda, to be followed by flannel hoods soaked in sodium hyposulphite. Eventually, Henry would have been issued with a gas helmet which had eyepieces and a respirator. As soon as the alarm was raised by the cry of 'gas, gas', the men would put on whatever protective equipment in use and would remain wearing it until the threat had passed. Gas attacks and respirators were another aspect of warfare that had to be adapted to, and which added to the stress of war. Survivors of gas attacks were invariably left with a weakness in their lungs for the rest of their lives.

The first use of poison gas by the Germans occurred on 22 April at Langemarck, which is north-east of Ypres. This part of the line was held by French colonial troops of the 45th (Algerian) Division, and the French 87th (Territorial) Division (Brown, 2001). These men were horribly unprepared for this form of warfare and unsurprisingly broke and ran, leaving a 4-mile gap in the line, giving the Germans an open approach to Ypres. In the documentary *We Await the Heavenly Manna*, one of the veterans interviewed speaks of receiving orders to rally the retreating French troops or failing that to shoot them, and he confirms that the orders were carried out.

Luckily for the Allies, the Germans failed to take advantage of this turn of events as they themselves were needing to be convinced that gas would be effective, and so had not, on this occasion, prepared for the next stage of such an attack. A major concern for the Germans was how advancing troops might be affected by this gas themselves.

Fortunately for the Allies the breach in the line was sealed by the Canadian 1st Division, who successfully secured a new forward defence line.

★★★

The Battle of Neuve Chappelle started on 10 March and finished on 12 March, and the 7th Division's battle orders read:

As soon as the village of Neuve Chappelle has been captured and made good, the 7th and 8th Divisions, supported by the Indian Corps on their right, will be ordered by the Corps Commander to press forward to capture the High Ground.

The battle started with a short thirty-five-minute bombardment of the German positions at 7.30 a.m., and the troops moved forward at 8.05 a.m. By 9 a.m. the village was captured, with the British finding the Germans surprised and their defences weakly held. Unfortunately, due to lack of an efficient communication system, the High Command learned of the successes much later and further advances were delayed, thereby allowing the Germans to bring up reserves. As a result, the line stabilised and deadlock returned, with each side suffering 11,000 casualties (Ashworth, 2000).

Henry may not have left a diary but his likely experience of Neuve Chappelle can be taken from some extracts from the diary of Lieutenant J.D. Wyatt of the 2nd Battalion in Brown (2001):

10 March. At about 8.45 we were told the front German trench had been carried and soon after the Brigade began to move off. We got to our old trenches at about 10.00 and really one couldn't make out what was going on. On the right prisoners were coming in streams, but we were not allowed to advance. And there we remained with nothing in front of us till 2pm. At 2pm we advanced and meeting with feeble resistance to our front but losing somewhat from enfilade fire from our right flank, we went on until dusk. Then we were told to dig ourselves in and there we stayed. There was little in front of us then but it was no good. The CO had orders to go no further. So we started making a trench. At 18 inches we came to water so had to content ourselves making a breastwork.

11 March. We held on to our position all day. The troops on our right were counter-attacked but not we fortunately as we were rather thin. We lost a few men that day by sniping from our right flank.

12 March. That night the Germans counter-attacked heavily on the right and got up a lot of guns. During the day we got our first taste of shelling. I gather one shell burst close to me and that ended my interest in the battle. I vaguely remember lying at the bottom of a shallow trench and then, when it grew dark, being told by someone to go and find a doctor.

Lieutenant Wyatt's wounds were bad enough for him to be returned to Britain.

★★★

Henry would have experienced going over the top and out of the relative security of the trenches, to be faced once again with mud, filth, sniping, machine guns, rifle fire, loud and sustained noise, spouts of earth shooting up in the air as shells landed, and atrocious conditions with water in the bottom of the shell holes – and survived, whilst many of his comrades would have been wounded and killed around him.

★★★

On 9 May 1915, the division was involved in the attack on Aubers Ridge where they came up against much stronger German defences involving deep dugouts, thick barbed wire and concrete machine-gun emplacements. The short barrage that preceded the attack was ineffective and the attack was called off after twelve hours, with the Allied soldiers decimated and a further 11,000 casualties.

Nevertheless, the British decided to assault Festubert to support the French fighting at Vimy Ridge, but this time after a four-day artillery barrage. Fighting started on 15 May and saw the 7th Division advance 500 yards into the German lines, but the long artillery barrage had given the Germans time to bring up their reserves and the advance stalled. Fighting continued until 27 May with the gain of one German line at a cost of 16,000 men.

In September the division was assigned to take part in the Battle of Loos. The German lines were well entrenched, yet Sir Douglas Haig, commanding this offensive, was sure he saw a German weakness in troop strength (Groom, 2003). However, when the advance started on the 26th, with 75,000 troops leaving their trenches at 6.50 a.m., it met with some initial success before the British repeatedly found themselves held up by machine-gun fire and artillery.

A good idea of what the troops faced can be gained from the following excerpt taken from the history of the German 26th Infantry Regiment (Holmes, 2005):

Never had machine guns had such straightforward work to do, or done it so effectively; with barrels burning hot and swimming in oil, they traversed to and fro along the enemy's ranks unceasingly: one machine gun alone fired 12,500 rounds that afternoon. The effect was devastating. The enemy could be seen literally falling in hundreds, but they continued to march in good order and without interruption. The extended lines of men began to get confused by this terrific punishment, but they went doggedly on, some even reaching the wire entanglement in front of the reserve line, which their artillery had scarcely touched. Confronted by this impenetrable obstacle, the survivors turned and began to retire.

The advance was not helped by an earlier release of cloud gas by the British that had lingered due to a gentler than expected breeze. Major General Capper went forward himself to view the situation but, sadly, was shot by a sniper and died the next day, having been taken to a casualty clearing station by his own retreating men.

The conditions faced by the advancing British were not ideal. They would be advancing through coal-mining country which was essentially flat and lacking in shelter, necessitating the use of smoke to screen the attack from the Germans. In addition, the reserve divisions were not sent forward by Sir John French (commanding the British Expeditionary Force) in good time. They had been held too far to the rear and were tired on arrival. Perhaps of greater impact on the troops and the success of the action, was the fact that the artillery simply did not have enough shells to put down an adequate barrage to disrupt the German defences and, in particular, destroy the barbed wire.

The Battle of Loos finally ended after a month and cost the division over 5,200 killed or wounded men.

On 20 December 1915, the brigade was transferred to the 30th Division, which formed part of Lord Kitchener's Fourth New Army.

HITLER IN 1915

By 17 February 1915, Adolf Hitler's division was located at Messines, and then in March it took part in the fighting at Neuve Chappelle (Williams, 2005), having marched for seven hours to Tourcoing, embarked on a train for Lille and marched from there.

On 10 March, the Bavarian Reserve Division was ordered to make a counter-attack but did not distinguish itself particularly well, with the Bavarian official history critical of the German organisation. On top of this, the division was deemed to have not performed particularly well in 1914, and so it would never again be used as a 'first line assault role' (Williams, 2005). This engagement resulted in a loss of twelve officers and 375 men, representing 23 per cent of all combat troops and 30 per cent of all combat officers.

The explanation (Weber, 2010) for this could be a wave of anti-Prussian feelings sweeping through the Bavarians. Hitler was to blame this on British propaganda rather than the harsh trench conditions and a pervading view that if it was not for the Prussians, the war would not have happened. It might be that this experience gave Hitler an insight into the power of propaganda.

Hitler's role was to convey messages between the regimental headquarters at Hapegards and the Bavarian assault battalions.

On 14 March, the regiment was relieved and sent to the trenches at Fromelles, where it was to hold a key position known as the Sugarloaf. This was a relatively quiet sector and it was only at night that there was any disturbance from enemy machine-gun or artillery fire. Casualty rates at this time were running at one man killed every thirty-six hours.

In a new position there were always many as yet unknown dangers, such as machine guns or snipers, and these hotspots would only become apparent over time. In this situation the popular view was that the first time a messenger was sent forward would be the most dangerous, and on 18 March Hitler was detailed to take that first message and survived. Weber, however, disputes the post-1920s/1930s versions of Hitler's wartime service. According to Weber, Hitler's duties as a despatch runner involved three shifts at the regimental headquarters inside Fromelles Castle, and three in the regular headquarters in Fournes, which was an hour's walk behind the lines. Hitler was therefore in danger from enemy artillery but no other weaponry.

Hitler, and his supporters, left a record that suggests that he was facing daily death moving from trench to trench, but again Weber argues that the reality was somewhat different. As a despatch runner for the regimental headquarters his job was to convey messages to the various battalion headquarters; it was the battalion despatch runners who went into the trenches.

Hitler was to claim that he had endured the same harsh trench conditions as the combat troops but the reality, according to Weber, was that he was ensconced in a comfortable billet behind the lines. Chapter 5 of Weber's book provides a compelling read which lays bare the embellishment of Hitler's wartime service and the reasons behind it.

At the end of April, the regiment was withdrawn and sent back for some R&R. The war took its toll on all participants and Kershaw gives the following description of Hitler:

> Photographs of him during the war show a thin, gaunt face dominated by a thick, dark, bushy moustache. He was usually on the edge of his group, expressionless where others were smiling.

Williams expands on this with the following description of Hitler in the years 1915–16 taken from photos of that time:

Show a gangling form in a baggy uniform. A serious looking, narrow head topped off his lop-sided stance, his facial features dominated by a sometimes straggly, sometimes Kaiser-like, and sometimes droopy moustache.

In May, the regiment fought at Aubers Ridge, which the British were unable to take despite having exploded two large mines under the German front line. The shock of the mines had allowed the British to advance, but the regiment regrouped and by 10 May re-took the ground that had been lost. This action resulted in 309 men killed and total casualties of 600.

★★★

From March to May, therefore, Henry and Adolf Hitler were again in close proximity to each other. At Neuve Chappelle, Lieutenant Wyatt's diary entry for 11 March tells of the troops to his right being counter-attacked – could this have been Hitler's regiment?

The British 7th Division unsuccessfully attacked Aubers Ridge and failed to break through the strong German defences where Hitler's regiment played its part. How close to each other may they have been at this time?

In either case, Hitler would not have been directly involved in the fighting but he would have been carrying messages to and from the front, and would have been a definite target for the British as they sought to disrupt the German communications.

1916

The 30th Division was originally the 37th which had formed part of the Fifth New Army, which, following a re-structuring, became the Fourth New Army. After a period of training the division was to be found in Grantham, and by October it had moved to Salisbury Plain. Lord Derby inspected the division on 4 November, after which it was transported to France, arriving by 12 November 1915 in the Amiens area, which is where Henry joined it. In March 1916, the Fourth Army had a new commander in General Sir Henry Rawlinson.

The year 1916 will be forever remembered for the Battle of the Somme, which started on 1 July and ended on 21 November and was fought with the sole purpose of relieving the pressure on the French at Verdun. This was to be a battle of attack and counter-attack that was to lead to the men on both sides being forced to live like animals, scrounging food and water, even from the bodies of those killed. It was to be a battle of the power of lead and iron against soft human flesh. The Battle of the Somme was a killing machine and as a result men were fed into the fighting, and such were the casualty rates that many never became known to those they fought with.

The battle started on 1 July and by the end of that day there were 57,470 British casualties, of which 19,240 were killed, which is roughly equivalent to the population of a small town. It is hard to imagine what it must have felt like waiting for the officers' whistles to blow and to go over the top, before walking into the hail of machine-gun bullets. Even worse would have been the sight of the first wave of soldiers mown down and to know that your turn to advance was about to come. What must have been going through the men's, and in particular Henry's, minds. And what could possibly make a man climb out of a trench and walk towards the enemy, having seen what had gone before? The reasons why men rose up out of the trenches and advanced towards the enemy were a mixture of bravery, a sense of not wanting to let the side down and the knowledge that to refuse would have dire consequences.

George Ashurst of the Lancashire Fusiliers described (1987, in Bird et al., 2008) what it was like going over the top on 1 July:

When we reached the front line trench there was no need to climb out on top. It was already battered flat and our wire entanglements blown to fragments. Instantly I jumped on top and ran as fast as I could through the powder smoke towards the sunken road, two thirds of the way across no-man's land, holding my head as I ran to shield my face as much as possible with my tin hat. The bullets made a horrible hissing noise all around me: shrapnel shells seemed to rend the sky and huge shells screamed down on us, shaking the ground under my feet and blowing to pieces both dead and wounded men who were lying about. Even in that mad dash I could hear the sickly thud as a bullet struck some comrade close by me, and every moment I fully expected a bullet to tear through my body.

From 1–13 July, Henry would have been involved in the Battle of Albert. Moving up to the front, Henry, a Roman Catholic, would have marched through the heavily damaged town of Albert, which had been a place of pilgrimage for Catholics. As they marched through the town the troops would have looked up at the golden statue of the Madonna and Child on top of the basilica. Despite heavy shelling and damage to its plinth, the statue, although now at a 120-degree angle, had not collapsed. The statue carried some significance to soldiers at the time, who believed that if it fell then the war would end. The British Army was also aware of this and so at night, and unknown to the soldiers, had engineers working to ensure the statue did not collapse (Gilbert, 2007).

October brought heavy rain, which in turn produced thick mud that was tiring to walk through. Everything that moved sank into the mud, whether it was men, animals, guns or vehicles. On 7 October, the Fourth New Army attacked the Transloy Ridge, which Philpott (2009) described as a lattice of trenches, gun positions and strong points that 'made little sense to the troops on the ground' in an attempt to take the village of Le Sars. To approach the ridge the troops had to advance through land that was overlooked by the Germans up on the ridge and – not surprisingly – it was unsuccessful.

A further attempt was made on 18 October with the attack starting at 3.45 a.m. The prevailing bad weather made effective artillery support difficult but nevertheless some 1,000 German prisoners were taken. But again the overall success was limited.

Macdonald (*The Roses of No Man's Land*, 1993) describes how the Germans had prepared for the British advance and:

Were spread out in a series of undetectable outposts, and immediately the machine guns began firing in unison from the Transloy Ridges far beyond the reach of the unwitting British field gunners. The bullets spat like hailstones on the parapet, and as the men left the trenches they advanced into a curtain of fire.

★★★

It was during the October actions that Henry was wounded in the leg, his first wound since being sent to the Western Front in October 1914. In that respect, Henry had been lucky, as the average was in the region of three months' service at the front before a soldier was either wounded or killed. Although details are scant, an article in the *Coventry Standard* (4 October 1963) reported that he had been shot through the calf, and two further bullets had passed through the back of his knee. It is not known how serious these wounds would have been but they constituted what the soldiers referred to as a 'blighty', a wound that was serious enough to see the individual removed from the front line, and in this case it necessitated his evacuation to a military hospital in England. But even receiving a blighty wound carried with it significant risks to survival due to the possibility of infection, disease and a lack of sterile conditions. The absence of antibiotics or a delay in receiving treatment meant that even a minor wound could lead to amputation of a wounded limb. According to Winter (1979), nearly all shell wounds went septic 'because of the foreign matter taken into the body with the splinters,' leading to a risk of gangrene.

There was a procedure, or what Doyle refers to as the 'casualty chain', which Henry would have entered, for getting a wounded man away from the battlefield, and, if required, to hospital in Britain, which was led by the Royal Army Medical Corps (RAMC). For this whole process to work it was dependent on the arrangements made and the manpower available in the context of battlefield conditions. This is brought to life in a quote from Lieutenant Harry Yoxall of the 18th Battalion, King's Royal Rifles (Brown, 2001):

Arrangements for the wounded are bad. Battalion Aid Posts are all in pill-boxes which have been taken from the enemy in the last few days. The stretcher bearers have got to bring the wounded from the First Aid Posts to the Mine Shaft, where they are redressed and then carried down to St Jean Corner, a distance of about a mile. At St Jean the wounded are placed in motor ambulances and conveyed to Red Farm from which they are finally shifted to the Casualty Clearing Station.

Other entries in Lieutenant Yoxall's diaries reveal the hardships experienced by the wounded and those who tended to them:

> Today was awful: was obliged to carry some of the wounded onto the graveyard and look on helpless till they died. Sometimes we could not even obtain a drink of water for them.
>
> Bringing wounded down from the front line today. Conditions terrible. The ground … is simply a quagmire. There is neither the appearance of a road or a path and it requires six men to every stretcher, two of these being constantly employed helping the others out of the holes; the mud in some cases up to our waists. A couple of journeys to and from the Mine Shaft and the strongest men are ready to collapse.

At first Henry would have made his own way, helped by another soldier or taken by a stretcher party to a regimental aid post located close to the front line, where he would have been seen by the regimental or battalion doctor providing a triage service. This may not have been straightforward depending on what was happening at the time in terms of movement of troops, any on-going action and the state of the trenches.

Evacuation by stretcher was a very labour-intensive activity requiring up to six bearers who may at times have been German prisoners of war. It was also the case that the evacuation of the wounded through the trenches took third place behind the movement of ammunition and reinforcements.

The regimental aid post would be located as close to the scene of any action as possible, perhaps in the cellar of a ruined house, a deserted dugout or a protected space to the side of a communications trench. It was here that dressings would be changed and if necessary arms or legs would be amputated (Winter), and a morphine or tetanus injection was given as required. Each soldier's pay book would be used for record purposes, and a label giving details of the case would be attached to a tunic button. The labels were placed into coloured covers to help inform those receiving the wounded at the next stage of the chain – a red cover would denote the more serious cases.

Those casualties, including Henry, who needed further treatment would then be taken to an advanced dressing station, either making their own way or by stretcher, to await evacuation by ambulance to the main dressing station. The dressing station would be located close to a road to allow for evacuation by wheeled vehicles, and, therefore, were at risk of coming under enemy shell fire. At all stages of the chain, wherever possible, movements were carried out at night to minimise the danger of both the wounded and those moving them being subjected to enemy fire. A wounded soldier's relief at being evacuated must, at times, have been sorely tested as they were unintentionally bounced and jerked around on stretchers and in the back of ambulances, but there was no other way it could have been done.

The next stage would see casualties moved further to the rear to casualty clearing stations, and then on to general or stationary hospitals. The casualty clearing stations were grim places and getting treatment took time. They were, in effect, a battleground accident and emergency department, with the walking wounded sitting around and the more serious cases lying on stretchers. It was not unusual for those wounded to die of shock, heart failure or loss of blood due to a lack of blood transfusions or sufficient operating theatres to deal with their wounds. This was despite the knowledge that if all dead and injured tissue was removed within thirty hours of damage it would help to control the onset of gangrene and sepsis (Winter). It would have been at the casualty clearing station that Henry would have had his wounds operated on.

The conditions in a casualty clearing station are described by Macdonald (1993):

> In some operating theatres at the heart of the push, two surgeons would be working at four to six operating tables, moving from one to the other, leaving often unqualified assistants to handle routine tasks of stitching up, dressing, and even anaesthetising, while they concentrated on the more delicate work of repairing damaged organs and searching for shrapnel, bullets, and shell splinters buried deep in muddy wounds.

Also, at all times it must be considered that the surgeons were operating without the knowledge, techniques, equipment and drugs that are routinely available today. There was, for example, no use of x-rays, leading to bullets or shell splinters remaining in the body, only to cause problems in later life.

Those 'lucky' casualties with a blighty were then transported back to hospitals in Britain. The first part of this journey would be by ambulance train, although sometimes barges or vehicle convoys would be used. The ambulance train allowed for large numbers of men to be moved but there was no way of keeping them warm, and provided little space for staff to tend to the casualties. Barges tended to be used for those casualties who could not be subjected to any form of shaking, but their use was dependent on the proximity of the casualty clearing station to a canal.

The final leg of the journey back to England would be by ship to ports such as Dover on the south coast. This was not a risk-free stage of the casualty chain either, as a number of hospital ships were sunk as a result of hitting a mine or being damaged by torpedo. The last leg of the journey would be by train to London, and then hospital.

The number of available hospitals was increased to cope with the numbers of casualties by utilising large country houses or public buildings such as schools, staffed by volunteer nurses from the Voluntary Aid Detachments.

It was not unusual for troops returning from the front, wounded or otherwise, to be met at the mainline London railway stations by large crowds, who cheered and threw cigarettes to them. On arriving at a hospital, Henry would have been issued with a new uniform of a blue suit worn with a red tie, which would have served as a form of status symbol denoting the wearer as having been wounded in the service of their country.

Henry survived both his wounds and his journey along the casualty chain, but he would not be considered fit to return to active service until May 1917, when he join the 3rd Battalion of the Green Howards. It was not be Henry's last experience of the casualty chain.

HITLER IN 1916

Up until the summer, 1916 was to be a relatively quiet period for the List Regiment. The German authorities were concerned about the 'soundness' of the regiment, and sought to raise morale by providing Munich beer and encouraging the men to visit the towns and villages behind the lines.

Weber tells of Hitler and his comrades taking the tram to Lille and attending performances by the Deutsches Theater Lille that had been set up in the Theatre de L'Opera in 1915. However, away from the theatre, the men wanted to drink and womanise, but not Hitler, who would wander the streets and sketch. Hitler was a committed teetotaller and had no interest in sleeping with local women, leading to speculation among his comrades that he was a homosexual.

The German Army, as did the British Army, took the prevalence of sexually transmitted diseases very seriously but chose to manage it in a different way. The German soldiers were issued with condoms and their names recorded so that the authorities could identify and punish those soldiers who had to be treated for a sexually transmitted disease in base hospitals.

Hitler's role as a regimental headquarters despatch runner precludes him from being viewed as a combat soldier, and as a result he did not share the life of those in the trenches. Weber states that Hitler more closely identified with his 'family' of regimental headquarters staff, made up of four officers and fifty other ranks, and in particular he delighted in the company of a dog, Foxl, who had belonged to a British unit.

In *Mein Kampf*, Hitler later claimed that he would have political discussions with his comrades, but Weber says that there is no evidence from those who served with him that this was the case.

The List Regiment was fortunate not to be sent directly to the Somme that summer but instead found itself guarding a quiet sector near Lille. Unbeknown to the Germans, the British chose to make a diversionary attack where the List Regiment was in place. The attack was ultimately unsuccessful but came at the cost of 340 casualties, of which 107 were killed.

On 29 September, the regiment was ordered to the Somme and arrived on 2 October. Initially, the work involved building a new set of defences at Bapaume, but then it took part in the defence of the Butte de Warlancourt in the unpleasant conditions caused by heavy rain. The regimental headquarters was set up in the village of La Barque, 1.2 miles from the front. It was here that Hitler was wounded in the left thigh, leading to another round of myth and counter-myth. According to Weber, the regimental records show that it was a light wound, received on 5 October, which nevertheless required him to be sent to a military hospital in Beelitz near Berlin, where he remained until 1 December. The wound was caused by a shell splinter from an explosion outside the entrance to the despatch runners' dugout at La Barque, not at a dugout at the front. On discharge from hospital Hitler was sent to the reserve unit of the regiment in Munich, where he stayed until March 1917.

The myths centre on him receiving a wound to the abdomen which cost him a testicle, and having been found on the battlefield by German Army medics as he lay there screaming and covered in blood. Weber questions why those who claimed to have found Hitler knew who he was, let alone who he was to become. In his own recollection of the episode, Hitler claims in *Mein Kampf* to have exhibited far greater bravery and closeness to the fighting than was the case, and manages to avoid mentioning that he was a despatch runner, and especially a regimental despatch runner.

Hitler therefore spent no more than four days on the Somme, while the regiment incurred large numbers of casualties, given by Williams as seven officers, 243 NCOs and men killed, and seventeen officers and 827 NCOs and men wounded. There were also a further two officers and eighty-eight men reported missing.

★★★

Both Henry and Hitler received their first wounds in October at the Somme, which necessitated time in hospital back in their respective home countries. Unlike Hitler, Henry had clearly been in the thick of the action, as had been the case since the later part of 1914.

1917

Henry was finally declared fit enough to return to duty and, following his discharge from hospital on 5 May, he joined the 3rd Battalion, Green Howards. The 3rd Battalion was a reserve battalion that remained in Richmond, Yorkshire, throughout the war, and its primary task was to provide drafts for other battalions. Soldiers who, through wounds or illness, had to be hospitalised did not automatically re-join their original battalion, and when fit were sent to help bring the other regimental battalions up to strength. While the regimental depot remained in Richmond, the battalion itself had moved to Hartlepool, which is where Henry joined it on 5 May 1917, and stayed there until 10 June when he transferred to the 9th Battalion in Flanders.

Henry took part in the Battle of Passchendaele, also known as the Third Battle of Ypres, which started on 31 July and finally ended on 16 November. The battle was also given the unofficial name of the 'Campaign of the Mud' because it was fought over land that was little more than a swamp. In Brown (2001) there is a quotation from Major C.E.L. Lynne (Royal Field Artillery) in which he describes Passchendaele as 'absolutely the most unholy spot from the North

Sea to the Mediterranean' because of the appalling conditions which had a debilitating effect on the morale of the troops.

The water table was only 2–3ft below the surface, so success was going to be weather dependent. Unfortunately, heavy rain fell, and combined with the effects of artillery shelling this left Henry and his comrades fighting through a very difficult terrain. Some men lost their boots in the mud and had to walk barefooted. The only way to get about was on wet and slippery duckboards, and men who fell off them drowned in the mud, sucked down under the weight of their equipment. Shell holes and craters were to be found either side of the duckboards, full of foul liquid containing the bodies of men, horses and mules. The mud was thick, cloying and everywhere. Everything and everyone soon became covered in mud. As much as a shell could vaporise a human body, many of those described as 'missing in action' would simply have disappeared below the mud. The men were often as afraid of drowning as they were of being shot.

The advantages of advancing behind a creeping barrage were lost as the soldiers became bogged down in the mud, unable to keep up. As a result, the Germans were able to emerge from their dugouts and fire on the advancing men once the barrage had passed. The unceasing rain had held the British up, allowing the Germans to regroup and regain the ground that had been lost.

The battle, as such, ended on 6 November when the Canadians took Passchendaele Ridge. This was followed on 20 November by further success at the Battle of Cambrai, made famous as the first battle to involve tanks *en masse*, when 400 of them caused a breakthrough of the German lines and a 5-mile advance. The blight affecting earlier advances struck again and the momentum of the attack was lost; on 30 November the Germans mounted a counter-attack causing the British to concede hard-won ground once again.

Henry was, by this time, out of the line having suffered his second wound of the war, on or about 27 November. There are no details of the nature of this wound other than that it was in an upper or lower limb, but it was serious enough for Henry to make a repeat journey through the various stages of the casualty chain, leading to another spell in hospital. He would not be fit enough to return to service until 23 January 1918, when he re-joined the 3rd Battalion.

The effect of participating in this battle was to leave the British Army depressed, as there seemed to be no end in sight to this war of continuous slaughter.

HITLER IN 1917

As with Henry, Hitler started 1917 on light duties following the wound he had received in October 1916. He returned to his regiment on 1st March, when it was based in Picardy, a few miles north of Vimy (Kershaw, 1998). Hitler had originally been ordered to report to the 2nd Bavarian Regiment, but he desperately wanted to go back to what he saw as his family – the List Regiment. Somehow he was able to make his case to its adjutant, Captain Weidemann, and he returned to his old position at regimental headquarters.

On 9 April the Canadians made a successful assault on Vimy Ridge, and the List Regiment was involved in the German response to the ensuing Allied breakthrough, which reached 6 miles. At one point, according to Weber, the British broke through the line held by the List Regiment with some eighty men and machine guns, which enabled them to fire on the regiment from behind. The machine guns were dealt with by grenades and the British withdrew.

The regiment had enjoyed some small success, which helped to produce a slight improvement in morale, but by early June it found itself enduring artillery and gas attacks. This led to its withdrawal back into Belgium, near Gheluvelt, where the regiment enjoyed a relatively quiet spell that was broken when the Allies began a ten-day bombardment, leading to 800 casualties. The improvement in morale did not last long and the regiment, at the request of its own commanding officer, was withdrawn on 24 July, returning to the Ypres Salient on the 27th. The expected British attack did not materialise and so two of the regiment's battalions were withdrawn, leaving behind the 2nd Battalion, including Hitler. But the attack did come and the 2nd Battalion had to face the first day of the British attack that was to become known as the Battle of Passchendaele.

The 2nd Battalion was then withdrawn to probably (Weber) the most peaceful area of the Western Front, which was west of Mulhausen on German soil. It was during this move that Hitler and his dog, Foxl, became separated, which caused Hitler more anguish than the decimation of his regiment.

As autumn approached, Hitler was awarded the Bavarian Military Medal of Honour Third Class, and it was then that he made his first ever application for leave. Leave represented an opportunity to return to see family and friends, but the regiment was Hitler's family, so for him this meant that he had no one to go to. Consequently, he embarked on a number of tourist visits to Brussels, Cologne, Dresden and Leipzig. He then moved on to Berlin, where he stayed until 7 October, and Weber points out that when he did write, it was a handful of postcards to regimental colleagues.

That autumn, the regiment was still understrength and fit only for defensive, as opposed to offensive, duties. It then moved back into France and took up position near Rheims, which is where Hitler re-joined regimental headquarters. On the night of 25/26 October the regiment was guarding the northern bank of the Oise-Aisne canal, where the terrain was swampy and there were no prepared positions. Initially, the regimental headquarters were located in a cave but was then relocated to a forest. The French then opened up an artillery barrage on the German lines, and it was at this time, with his men under fire, that the regiment's commanding officer, Anton von Tubuef, decided to go hunting in the forest (Weber). He chose to use the men of the support staff, including Hitler, to act as beaters, leading Weber to comment that 'the primary danger Hitler had to face was posed by wild boars'.

Eventually the fighting died down and the regiment enjoyed a relatively quiet period up to and over what was to prove to be the last Christmas of the war.

★★★

The year 1917 saw both Henry and Hitler involved in the Battle of Passchendaele, but they had very different experiences. Henry had been in the thick of the fighting, which had led to him receiving a further wound and repatriation to England.

Where Hitler seemed to have been caught up in the action, albeit brief, it resulted from simple bad luck, but he had still escaped injury. Hitler's war of 1917 saw him take leave and enjoy a period of tourism, and take part in his commanding officer's boar hunt. It would be easy to make much of this, but, for whatever reason, he was serving in a regiment in a capacity that was less dangerous than that of a front-line soldier – can he really be blamed for taking advantage of that? He could so easily have found himself in another regiment where his war would have been different and probably shorter.

1918

On being declared fit to serve, Henry was discharged from hospital and this time joined the 12th Battalion in France in 1918, and when this was disbanded in July 1918, Henry joined the 5th Duke of Wellington's Regiment, in which he served from 26 July until 4 October 1918 as Private Henry Tandy (No. 34506). It was during this period that Henry was awarded the three highest awards for bravery, starting with the Distinguished Conduct Medal (DCM) on 28 August at Vaulx Vraucourt. In an article in the *Coventry Evening Telegraph* in 1997, he is reported to have said the following about his exploits:

> Somehow I never thought I should get killed. During the fighting I never knew what time it was or even what day it was, and I spent two years in the trenches before I was hit.

It is impossible to know whether that was really what Henry felt during the war or not. Brown (2001) quotes from a letter from Second Lieutenant Edward Beddington-Behrens to his sister, in which he wrote:

Do you know, I feel that I am going to get killed in this war, this feeling has almost reached a dead certainty lately.

However, Second Lieutenant Edward Beddington-Behrens survived the war, only to say in later life 'that he had always been convinced that he would survive'. These are two irreconcilable views which serve to highlight the tricks that the passage of time can play on the memory, but may also demonstrate someone trying to mask from family and friends the horrors and mental torture he had experienced.

It is possible that Henry had genuinely held that conviction throughout his time on the Western Front, and if he did then the probability is that it would have stemmed from his Catholic faith. The majority of both officers and men, on both sides, tended to put their trust in God to see them through the war. Church parade on a Sunday was compulsory for all men, whatever their beliefs, and this would have been less of an imposition for Henry than it might have been for others.

As a Roman Catholic, Henry would have seen more of the Catholic chaplains than those from other faiths because, unlike those from other faiths, they were encouraged to be in the front line to administer extreme unction. Army chaplains were given officer rank and carried out a range of duties, such as administering to the dead and dying, performing burials, giving troops absolution as they went forward, attempting to maintain morale and even censoring letters from the front.

Chaplains from other faiths tended not to go too near the front, leading some soldiers to feel that, although they might give a fire-and-brimstone speech exhorting the troops to advance and fight, they did not share the inherent dangers involved. This is captured nicely in a quotation (Holmes, 2005) from Siegfried Sassoon, who was unhappy with a particular chaplain's choice of words:

'And now God go with you' he had told a group of men bound for the front. 'I will go with you as far as the station.'

★★★

The DCM, created in 1854, was for distinguished service in the field for warrant officers, non-commissioned officers and the lower ranks, and was usually announced in the *London Gazette*, along with a citation. The citation for Henry's award, which he received for his actions from 25 August to 2 September 1918, appeared in the gazette on 5 December 1918:

> He was in charge of a reserve bombing party, in action, and finding the advance temporarily held up he called on two other men of his party, and working across the open in rear of the enemy, he rushed a post, returning with 20 prisoners, having killed several of the enemy. He was an example of daring courage throughout the whole of the operations.

Citations in the *London Gazette* sometimes tended to be briefer than the actual Recommendation for Awards for Gallantry. Henry's recommendation for the DCM was dated 5 October 1918, and was signed by Captain K. Sykes, adjutant of the 5th Battalion:

> For most determined bravery and initiative during operations from 25th August to 2nd September 1918, particularly during the attack on a system of trenches on 28th August. He was in charge of a reserve bombing party and finding the parties in front temporarily held up he called on the other 2 men of his party and worked across the open in rear of the enemy and rushed the post coming back with 20 prisoners, after having killed several of the enemy. His daring action and initiative largely contributed to the capture of the Northern Trench. He was an example of daring courage throughout the whole of the operations.

The additional detail reveals that the action took place at Havrincourt and that 28 August was the key date, with Henry's contribution significant in the capture of the Northern Trench. This was the occasion which resulted in the one exception to the lack of postcards or letters sent by Henry from the front. The Green Howards Regimental Museum has a postcard showing a group of German soldiers. Henry had taken the postcard from the pack of a captured German soldier and had written: 'Batch of prisoners I captured on winning the DCM. The post cards taken out of one of their packs.' Sadly no note has been taken of any addressee, nor is there any evidence that it was in fact posted.

The award of the Military Medal (MM), created in March 1916, was for distinguished service in the field by warrant officers, non-commissioned officers and the lower ranks, and again all awards were announced in the *London Gazette*. Henry's MM was for heroism at Havrincourt on 12 September 1918, and was announced in the *London Gazette* on 13 March 1919, the day that he received it, together with a summary of the reasons for the award:

> During an attack at Havrincourt on September 12th 1918, this man exhibited great heroism and devotion to duty. He went out under most heavy shell fire and carried a badly wounded man on his back. He then went out again and found three more wounded men and put them under cover and fetched a party of men to bring them in. During a bomb attack on the Hindenburg Line on September 13th he volunteered to be leading bomber and then led the party over the open. He made himself responsible for holding the bombing block in the trench and whilst doing this the post was attacked by the enemy in strength. The German officer shot at him point blank and missed. Private Tandey, quite regardless of danger, then led his party against the enemy and drove them away in confusion. This soldier's conduct was throughout of the highest order, and for gallantry and determined leadership beyond all praise.

On this occasion the announcement in the *London Gazette* repeats word for word the recommendation that Captain Sykes found himself writing on 15 October 1918.

The Victoria Cross (VC) is the highest British award for gallantry in the face of the enemy and was established in 1856. The process followed for giving such an award starts with a recommendation from the individual's regiment, supported by three independent eyewitness accounts. The process ends with a final submission for approval to the Secretary of State for War and the monarch. All awards of the VC were announced in the *London Gazette* and always with a citation.

Henry's award of the VC was announced in the *London Gazette* on 14 December 1918, and was awarded for conspicuous bravery at Marcoing, situated on the St Quentin canal, south-west of Cambrai, on 28 September 1918. The recommendation had been signed by Lieutenant Colonel Harold E. Lea of the 62nd (West Riding) Division.

The British attacked at 6.30 a.m., with the objective of advancing against Masnières on the Schelde canal. Little had happened until the village of Marcoing was reached, where the German machine-gunners had taken up position in the attics of the village buildings and were causing severe casualties among the advancing troops. This necessitated the advancing troops moving from house to house to flush them out.

The 5th Duke of Wellington's kept moving forward until they reached a canal. The canal presented a major obstacle, with machine-gun and rifle fire sweeping it from the front and sides and all the approach routes. In addition, all the bridges had been destroyed and its banks were very deep, presenting major difficulties for those seeking to cross it.

As a first step, the British sent its Lewis gunners to take up position in those attics recently cleared of their German counterparts. The commanders of B and D Companies then started to dribble men across the canal, but against such heavy enemy fire little significant progress could be made. Eventually, the 5th Battalion found itself alone on the German side of the canal, and in an increasingly precarious position with the enemy preparing to counter-attack.

The 5th Battalion was ordered to advance behind a creeping barrage. Initially this proved to be successful as the Germans were thrown into confusion, but it was not sustainable as the enemy still had a superior number of troops. The fighting took on the form of hand-to-hand combat and all four companies were soon weak in numbers.

During the fighting, Henry had led the destruction of a machine-gun position that was holding up the advance, and had replaced planks on a railway bridge that was under fire, to enable the British to cross the canal at that point. Gradually the position of the Duke of Wellington's Regiment became more and more precarious, but a further advance behind a creeping barrage was timed for 6.15 p.m., some twelve hours after the initial advance. Henry was one of only eighteen men from A Company that had managed to reach the Marcoing Switch. Unfortunately, the other platoons could not keep up and although Henry's platoon, led by Second Lieutenant W.J. Lloyd, captured a machine gun, together with one German officer and eight men, it found itself surrounded. If the men were to avoid capture themselves then there was no other option but to fix bayonets, charge the enemy and break out that way. The ferocity of the attack shook the Germans involved and as a result the men broke out of their precarious position, capturing some thirty-seven Germans on the way. Henry was the only one of the British to be wounded and despite that he went on to capture a further twenty Germans.

The award citation reads as follows:

For desperate bravery and great initiative during the capture of the village and the crossings at Marcoing and the later counter-attack on September 28, 1918. During the advance on Marcoing this soldier's platoon was held up by machine gun fire and stopped. He at once crawled forward under heavy fire, located the machine gun position, led a Lewis gun team into a neighbouring house from which they were able to knock out the gun, and his platoon continued the advance. On arrival at the crossing the plank bridge was broken, and under heavy fire and seemingly impassable, he crawled forward, putting the planks into position and making the bridge passable under a hail of bullets, this enabling the first crossing to be made at this vital spot. He must have seen that the chances of losing his life amounted to almost a certainty. Later in the evening, during an attack by his company to enlarge the bridgehead and capture Marcoing support trench he with eight comrades, was surrounded by an overwhelming number of Germans, and though the position was apparently hopeless, he led a bayonet charge through them, fighting so fiercely that 37 of the enemy were driven into the hands of the remainder of his company and taken prisoner, the party winning clear though he was twice wounded. Even then he refused to leave, leading parties into dug-outs and capturing over 20 of the enemy, and though faint from loss of blood, stayed till the fight was won.

The recommendation for the award was supported by eyewitness accounts from his platoon commander, Second Lieutenant W.J. Lloyd, and Private L. Lister. Private Lister gave his account as follows (Brereton and Savory, 1993):

On 28th September 1918 during the taking of the crossing over the Canal de St. Quentin at Marcoing, I was No.1 of the Lewis gun team of my platoon. I witnessed the whole of the gallantry of Private Tandey throughout the day. Under intensely heavy fire he crawled forward in the village when we were held up by the enemy MG and found where it was, and then led myself and comrades with the gun into a house from where we were able to bring Lewis gun fire on the MG and Knock it out of action. Later when we got to the crossings and the bridge was down, Pte Tandey, under the fiercest aimed MG fire went forward and replaced planks over the bad part of the bridge to enable us all to cross without delay, which would otherwise have ensued. On the same evening when we made another attack we were completely surrounded by Germans, and we thought the position might be lost. Pte Tandey, without hesitation, though he was twice wounded very nastily, took the leading part in our bayonet charge on the enemy, to get clear. Though absolutely faint he refused to leave us until we had completely finished our job, collected our prisoners and restored the line.

Henry was shot both in a leg and an arm and his wounds, which were described by Private Lister as very nasty, necessitated a period of hospitalisation in England.

The end of that day would have found Henry wounded, bleeding and in pain, tired and almost certainly surprised to have survived. At that moment, Henry would have been unaware of two developments that were to impact on his life. Firstly, he would have had no idea that he would be recommended for, let alone be awarded, the VC. Secondly, twenty years would pass before he learned that on the day he had won the most prestigious military award he had also, apparently, through an act of compassion, saved the life of the future architect of the Second World War – Adolf Hitler.

It is a debatable point whether, as a result of these two developments, he is better known for his bravery or his act of compassion to the man who was to lead Germany into the next world war.

The story of Henry saving Hitler's life is simply that – a story – unless evidence can be found to substantiate it. Consequently, Chapter 5 will examine the evidence to establish whether or not the incident actually took place.

★★★

Henry was not discharged as fit to serve until March 1919, at which point he re-enlisted for a further three years with the 3rd Duke of Wellingtons based in Halifax.

Henry had steadfastly refused promotion throughout the war, saying that he had joined up to be a soldier, but he was recognised as a special type of soldier by his commanding officer, who gave him a roving commission after he had been decorated which excused him from parades, fatigues and drills. The *Leamington Spa Courier*, dated 20 December 1918, quoted the *Daily Telegraph* as describing Henry as 'a hero of the old berserk type'.

★★★

It is interesting to speculate, and it can be no more than speculation, about Henry's state of mind during this period of little more than a month, from 25 August until 28 September, during which his bravery received such recognition. Looking back on those events with the benefit of today's knowledge, it would be easy to say, with the end of the war just weeks away and having survived on the Western Front since 1914, why would anyone put their life at risk? The truth, though, is that Henry, as was the case with all those involved in the fighting, would not have known that the war was drawing to an end, and so was there something else fuelling the actions of this 'hero of the old berserk type'?

Between 1914 and 1918 Henry was Mentioned in Despatches (MID) no less than five times. An MID can be looked upon as a form of consolation prize for not receiving a gallantry award. This may well have frustrated Henry, who possibly saw others receive medals for doing no more, if not less, than him, and this seems to have been what lay behind his transfer to the Duke of Wellington's Regiment. Something certainly motivated him to request a transfer, and a clue may be in the following quotation taken from the *Green Howards Gazette* in April 1917, referring to the period from October 1914 to September 1916:

> While with the 2nd Battalion his name was on several occasions brought forward for gallantry but without result.

It could be that his commanding officer did not support a recommendation for a gallantry award, and being consistently ignored in this way simply irritated Henry, so that when the opportunity to transfer arose he jumped at the chance.

Henry was quoted in the *Iron Duke* in the spring of 1978, which contained his obituary, as making it clear that he felt a real affinity with the Duke of Wellington's that he had not felt with the Green Howards:

> He told me that before he came to this Battalion he felt he never had the chance to distinguish himself but amongst us Yorkshiremen he felt thoroughly at home, and at once felt the wonderful esprit de corps that existed, and he was determined to be a part of it and help it on – and well he did so.

Henry's friend, Clive Bacon, in a letter dated 30 November 1980, recalls that during a visit to Henry a few months before he died, Henry had said that he transferred from the Green Howards because he was unable to get any recognition for his actions.

This gives an interesting glimpse into Henry's character because his feelings while with the Green Howards show frustration and perhaps some jealously at others having their actions formally recognised by the award of medals.

Towards the end of his life Henry revealed, perhaps without recognising that he himself had been guilty of this or of his earlier sentiments, that he had felt that others in the regiment were jealous of him and his bravery awards, and perhaps of how he had been feted. The particular incident that triggered the jealousy appears to be an occasion when Henry was selected, over the claims of others, to carry the regimental colours. Henry's recollection seems at odds with the fact that he had been quite happy to re-enlist in the regiment on 15 March 1919, serving another seven years, under the then Lieutenant Colonel Keith Sykes who, in a letter reproduced in Henry's obituary carried in the *Green Howards Gazette* in spring 1978, describes him as:

> A most gallant fellow, and was loved by all with whom he came into contact.

The obituary then went on to include the following sentiment:

> When he obtained the VC it was wonderful to see how many of his comrades volunteered to give verbatim accounts of his wonderful conduct.

It is sad that Henry came to the end of his life feeling as he did about the Duke of Wellington's, but, perhaps, as revealed by the above quotation, it was not the award that aroused jealousy, but what his comrades then went on to see as the preferential treatment subsequently accorded to him by his commanding officer.

★★★

1. Henry's father James Tandy. (Courtesy of the Gordon family)

2. Henry's mother with her grandson Stanley. (Courtesy of the Gordon family)

3. School photograph, c. 1905. Henry is third from right in the front row. (Courtesy of St Peter's church, Leamington Spa)

4. The Regent Hotel, Leamington Spa, in about 1880. (Photograph by Francis Bedford, courtesy of Leamington Spa Picture Library)

5. One of the many houses wrecked by shell fire at the First Battle of Ypres, 1914. (*London Illustrated News*)

6. Private Henry Tandey in a painting of the Menin Crossroads in October 1914 by Fortunino Matania. Henry is in the right foreground carrying a wounded comrade to a first aid station. (Courtesy of the Green Howards Museum)

7. Above: British Vickers machine-gun crew wearing anti-gas helmets, near Ovillers during the Battle of the Somme, 1916. (Wikimedia Commons)

8. Left: Henry (left) with the officer who he is depicted as carrying on his back in the Matania painting, and the officer's wife and daughter. (Courtesy of the Gordon family)

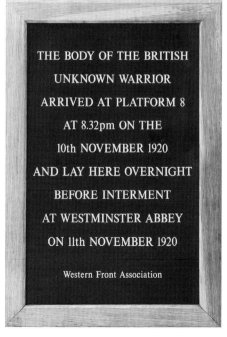

THE BODY OF THE BRITISH
UNKNOWN WARRIOR
ARRIVED AT PLATFORM 8
AT 8.32pm ON THE
10th NOVEMBER 1920
AND LAY HERE OVERNIGHT
BEFORE INTERMENT
AT WESTMINSTER ABBEY
ON 11th NOVEMBER 1920

Western Front Association

9. Henry Tandey in uniform with his medals superimposed. (Courtesy of the Gordon family)

10. Plaque at Victoria station showing where the body of the Unknown Warrior lay the night before internment at Westminster Abbey. (Author's photograph)

11. The Canadians on Passchendaele Ridge, firing and bombing a pillbox. (*London Illustrated News*)

12. Henry's Victoria Cross. (Courtesy of the Green Howards Museum)

13. Henry on parade, standing in the middle, probably in either Egypt or Turkey during the period 1919–26. (Courtesy of the Gordon family)

14. Hitler (indicated by white cross) with other soldiers in the First World War. (US National Archives)

15. The 1963 Green Howards reunion at the Queen Elizabeth Barracks at Strensall near York. Henry is second from left. (Courtesy of the Green Howards Museum)

16. The wedding of Leslie, Henry Tandey's nephew, in 1964. Henry is sixth from the right. (Courtesy of the Gordon family)

17. Adolf Hitler as Führer during the Second World War. (*London Illustrated News*)

18. Henry and his brother George attending a function in London in the 1960s. (Courtesy of the Gordon family)

19. A French official preparing to bury Henry's ashes at the Masnières British Cemetery near Marcoing. (Courtesy of the Gordon family)

20. Henry's illuminated scroll giving him Freedom of the Borough of Royal Leamington Spa. (Author's photograph)

21. December 1976: Henry, aged 85, holding his medals at the Walsgrave Hospital, Coventry. (Courtesy of Michael Crumplin FRCS)

22. Right: Henry Tandey's dress medals. (Author's photograph)

23. Below: Henry Tandey's original medal ribbons. (Author's photograph)

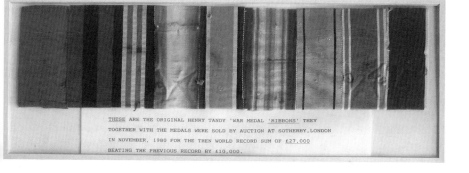

THESE ARE THE ORIGINAL HENRY TANDY 'WAR MEDAL 'RIBBONS' THEY
TOGETHER WITH THE MEDALS WERE SOLD BY AUCTION AT SOTHERBY, LONDON
IN NOVEMBER, 1980 FOR THE THEN WORLD RECORD SUM OF £27,000
BEATING THE PREVIOUS RECORD BY £10,000.

24. Freemen of the Borough of Royal Leamington Spa. (Author's photograph)

25. The gold-plated casket and scroll presented to Henry in 1919 when he was made a Freeman of the Borough of Royal Leamington Spa. (Author's photograph)

26. Henry's medals being presented to the now General the Lord Dannatt at a ceremony at the Tower of London in 1997. Also present are Sir Ernest Harrison (middle) and Henry Gordon (left). (Courtesy of the Gordon family)

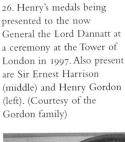

27. The clock presented to Henry Tandey by the Old Contemptibles' Association. (Courtesy of the Gordon family)

Unfortunately, as has already been said, there are no surviving diaries or letters belonging to Henry and so they cannot be used as indicators of how he was feeling. One possibility is that he had simply had enough; he was at the end of his tether, saw no end to the war and, therefore, had stopped worrying about his own self-preservation – in other words he was beyond caring.

Frank Richardson, in his postscript to Babington's book, talks about the idea of a bank balance of courage, which needs time to be replenished, and that each time this is required it will not only take longer to do, but will not last as long, demonstrating that 'every soldier, however brave and resolute, has his breaking point'. Could this have been the case with Henry? Had he simply had enough and could not stand the thought of more fighting, bloodshed, trench life and another winter in the trenches?

Henry had seen active service on the Western Front since 1914 and was an experienced soldier, but maybe the cost of that was a man who was worn out. Military psychology, and an understanding of the mental well-being of soldiers, was in its infancy in the Great War and so soldiers were being allowed to wear themselves out because of military traditions, and ignorance, in the context of a war which made huge demands on those involved.

Perhaps Henry had had enough of seeing his comrades killed around him, as Harry Stephens of the 16th Battalion, Australian Infantry commented (Brown, 2001):

> When you see your dead comrades around it steels you to courage and makes you feel that you must hit him and hit him hard.

This could well have been how he felt, causing him to be fired up to exact a form of revenge on the Germans. Henry, acting as he did, clearly showed no fear, despite having been wounded in 1916 and 1917. He would have known what it felt like to be wounded, and he would have seen more than his share of death and mutilation, yet he still was prepared to lead a bayonet charge, crawl on to a bridge under enemy fire and rescue wounded comrades.

Williams makes the following interesting observation on bravery:

When Medals are awarded who can say if the recipient has conquered the fears within in an act of selfless devotion – or if he is unstable, suicidal, indulging in an act of crazy bravado.

As quoted earlier, Henry later said: 'Somehow I never thought I should get killed', and Richardson said that some soldiers, having conquered their fear, develop a 'tendency to show off a bit, deliberately displaying fearlessness in order to encourage others by example' – could this be an explanation for his actions? Henry had simply conquered his fear, and this provided him with the mental armour to allow him to display such extraordinary bravery and leadership.

Whatever was behind his actions on the three occasions that led to gallantry awards, it is clear that he was an exceptionally brave man and soldier. In fact, the army further recognised Henry's bravery by presenting him with a parchment that simply stated that any continued displays of bravery in the future could not be recognised, as there were no other awards in existence that could be presented to him.

HITLER IN 1918

Early 1918 saw Hitler and his regiment operating in Picardy and Champagne. Morale was still low, particularly as the men were hungry and the evidence of the food available to the British, when trenches were captured, caused many to realise the true state of affairs (Weber, 2010).

In March and April, the regiment, which was viewed as an auxiliary rather than a front-line unit, worked to set up a defence line near Montdidier to protect the territorial gains of the German Spring Offensive. According to Weber, the regiment suffered heavy losses, and by April had lost half its men through death, injury or illness. The regiment was relieved on 26 April, returning to the

Oise/Aisne sector on the 30th, where it took part in 'an attritional defensive action against a crack and much feared unit of French Zouaves' (Williams, 2005).

In May 1918, Hitler received two more commendations, firstly the Regimental Diploma for Outstanding Bravery and another for being wounded (Persico, 2005).

To add to the regiment's troubles it had to contend with an outbreak of Spanish flu in June, which was to cause many deaths throughout the rest of 1918 and beyond, not just to the troops of both sides but also on the home fronts too. Hitler's luck continued as he avoided catching this virus.

By 15 July, the regiment had its strength boosted by a replacement draft of 900 men, mostly made up of new recruits and those returning from periods out of the line with wounds or illness. Morale was still poor, as the regiment was involved in the Second Battle of the Marne, which failed in its objectives and thus ended the German chances of victory on the Western Front. Hitler, with his revisionist approach to the truth, later referred to this as a 'glorious and epic endeavour' on the part of the German Army (Weber, 2010).

In August, Hitler was awarded the Iron Cross First Class for his service since 1914 as a despatch runner. Weber contends that this was the incident that created the myth of Hitler as 'an heroic frontline soldier'. The Iron Cross First Class was the highest honour available to men of Hitler's rank in the German Army, and it was rarely awarded. It is argued by some that it demonstrates how dangerous the role of a despatch runner was, but this is something that Weber disputes. In his book, he points to the fact that those serving with Hitler as despatch runners in 1915 enjoyed a 100 per cent survival rate. Weber also points to a newspaper article written by Stettner in 1932, which states that the award was generally given to the support staff of regimental headquarters rather than to front-line troops, so the award given to Hitler was more as a result of his position and long service than bravery.

Hitler was nominated for the award by a Jewish officer by the name of Gutmann, a fact that was later edited out of Hitler's autobiography, and is said to be based on his delivery of a despatch to the front line under dangerous conditions. Weber quotes Hitler's regimental commander, Emmerich von Godin, who wrote:

> ... as a despatch runner he was a model in sangfroid and grit both in static and mobile warfare [and that] he was always prepared to volunteer to deliver messages in the most difficult situations under great risk to his own life.

This statement seems to support the view that the award was not for a single incident but more for services rendered over a period of time. In the hands of the Nazi propaganda machine, however, the story became that of true heroism, with Hitler taking prisoner a number of British soldiers, or in another version that he personally captured twelve French soldiers. Weber points out that the latter incident did actually take place, but rather than Hitler acting on his own, the entire regimental staff was involved.

★★★

Mid-August saw the regiment moved to Cambrai, where a British offensive was taking place near Bapaume, but, on the 21st, Hitler was sent for a week's telephone communications training near Nuremberg (Kershaw, 1998). As a result, Hitler was away from the front for most of what remained of the war. After the training he took leave in September and spent some time in Berlin. On his return, the regiment was under pressure from British assaults near Comines.

For Hitler, his war was drawing to an end, and in October the regiment was relocated to the Ypres sector, where on the night of the 13/14th he was temporarily blinded in a British mustard gas attack. According to Williams:

> He and several comrades, retreating from their dug-out during a gas attack, were partially blinded by the gas and found their way to safety

only by clinging to each other and following a comrade who was slightly less badly afflicted.

Hitler received initial treatment in Belgium before being moved to a military hospital in Pasewalk, Germany. Weber contends that Hitler was in fact treated for war hysteria, probably what today would be called post-traumatic stress, and where he was diagnosed as 'a psychopath with symptoms of hysteria'.

It was there that he heard news of the Armistice and was so upset that it brought on a reoccurrence of his blindness. His sight returned, and on 19 November he returned to Munich via Berlin, eventually being discharged from the German Army on 31 March 1920, and the rest, as they say, is history.

★★★

The similarities in the military service of both Henry and Hitler are remarkable. Both served throughout the war on the Western Front, received a number of wounds, and were recognised for bravery. In a remarkable coincidence, both were wounded as the war drew to a close, and were in hospital at its conclusion.

Despite Weber's revision of Hitler's military service, which argues that as a regimental headquarters despatch runner he had a softer war than those in the front line, any soldier from whichever side who served on the Western Front cannot have their service dismissed as being anything less than brave. It was just that some were braver than others, due to the desperate situations they found themselves in.

On 11 November 1918, the British prime minister, Lloyd George, told the House of Commons the conditions of the Armistice, and concluded by saying (Wilson, 2005):

Thus at eleven o'clock this morning came to an end the cruellest and most terrible war that has ever scourged mankind. I hope we may say that thus, this fateful morning, came to an end all wars.

Those were words that Henry would have been waiting a long time to hear because they meant an end to fighting, loss of life, mutilation and the attendant horrors of war. He would have been delighted to have survived and that the Allies had won.

Sadly, Hitler did not receive the news in that way, and on 9 November his view was made clear in a conversation he had with Captain Weidemann (Wilson, 2005), in which he chillingly said:

> Every generation needs its own war and I shall take care that this generation gets its war.

1919–26

The Mayor of Royal Leamington Spa, Councillor George Cashmore, sent a telegram to Henry on the award of his VC, saying:

> In the name of the inhabitants of the Borough, I offer you heartiest congratulations upon the great honour that has been conferred upon you by H.M. the King. You are the first Leamington man to win the coveted distinction, and the whole Town is proud of your achievements.

At the meeting of the General Purposes Committee of the Royal Borough of Leamington Spa, on 21 January 1919, it was decided to mark the 'heroic conduct' of Henry by conferring on him the Honorary Freedom of the Borough. There was also an approval of a motion to 'open a fund with a view to presenting him at the same time with a suitable testimonial'.

The *Daily Graphic* newspaper, on 24 January 1919, briefly reported that Henry had spent the previous weekend, his first since receiving his VC, at home in Leamington Spa, before returning to hospital. Henry was back when, on 27 February 1919, a ball was held at Urquart Hall, Leamington Spa, in aid of the Mayor's Fund for Tandey. The *Leamington Spa Courier* reported on the event, stating that shortly before 8 p.m. all 200 tickets had been purchased. The ballroom was 'brilliantly decorated with national flags and trophies, and the stage – occupied by the Standard Orchestra – was set off most attractively with palms and flowers'. Henry attended the ball and presented the prizes for the most attractive and original costumes worn.

When Henry was made a Freeman of the Borough of Royal Leamington Spa he was presented with a gold-plated casket containing a decorated scroll, as a result of the donations, which is now kept in the Mayor's Parlour in the town hall in Leamington Spa (plate 25).

In as far as Henry would have allowed himself to be viewed as a 'celebrity', there would only have been limited national awareness at the end of the war, of who he was and what he had achieved. Henry was undoubtedly an extraordinary man and soldier who had been awarded the VC, DCM and MM in just a matter of weeks in the late summer of 1918, but the times he lived in were very different to those of today, particularly in terms of media coverage and of the strict censorship of soldiers' letters and media coverage. It can only be imagined what the media of today would have made of a modern-day Private Henry Tandey VC DCM MM, and how he would almost certainly have become a national celebrity and a public face of the military.

If Henry was returning today from the war in Afghanistan, having been awarded the VC, DCM and MM, the sofas of breakfast television would beckon, together with appearances on other television and radio programmes; there would be newspaper and magazine interviews with photographic spreads, a very prominent role in that November's Royal British Legion's Festival of Remembrance at the Royal Albert Hall, and coverage of him receiving his awards from the Queen at Buckingham Palace. In today's world, those media events would be guaranteed. Based on the picture of Henry that has emerged from the available literature, and the recollections of his family, it is safe to say that Henry would have hated every minute of such exposure.

★★★

Henry was discharged from the army on 14 March 1919, but re-enlisted on 15 March 1919 on a short-term engagement into the 3rd Battalion of the Duke of Wellington's, on what was known as Home Service. He was subsequently posted to the 2nd Battalion on 4 February 1921, where he remained until his final army discharge on 5 January 1926.

Henry's decision to re-enlist having just survived four years on the Western Front may, at first glance, look surprising. He could have been forgiven for taking the opportunity to leave the army for life as a civilian, but Henry was a regular soldier and he enjoyed soldiering. It also demonstrates awareness, on Henry's part, that civilian life was, at that time, more uncertain, while the army represented an income and security.

It does perhaps seem surprising that he should choose to re-enlist with the Duke of Wellington's, given his comments about experiencing jealousy. This can be explained by the fact that, having been wounded on 28 September 1918, he spent little time between then and his re-enlistment with either his battalion or his regiment. Any jealously that he experienced must, therefore, have occurred between 1919 and 1926, after he had re-enlisted. Here he would have found himself not with those he knew in the 5th Battalion, but in battalions where he would have been less well-known, and where his special treatment may have been resented.

★★★

Henry received his VC from George V at an investiture held at Buckingham Palace on 17 December 1919, and the medal bears the simple inscription:

34506 PTE. H. TANDEY. D.C.M. M.M.

5TH BN. W. RID. R [TF]

28

SEP

1918

Around this time, a small article on Henry appeared in the *Halifax Guardian*, in which he said that he had been invited to a number of public functions but stated he would prefer going 'over the top' to 'any of these stunts'.

The article also said that Henry had been in Manchester, and experienced a curious incident:

> When he was pulled up by an officer who asked for an explanation of all these decorations. Fortunately he had a letter from the Records Office to prove his right to wear the ribbons, and then received the congratulations of the officer.

It is perhaps understandable that the officer, on seeing a full set of bravery awards pinned to the chest of a private soldier, would have been curious and quite within his rights to question the credentials of the individual concerned. Nevertheless, the officer was, on discovering that everything was in order, only too ready to offer his congratulations.

This was apparently a common occurrence for Henry according to a letter held at the Imperial War Museum from a W.H. Colley, dated 3 November 1997. In his letter, Mr Colley states that there was '… always an officer detailed to get him out of the guardroom, whither he was liable to be taken by the Military Police for wearing medals to which he was not entitled'. As irksome as this would have been for Henry, it does highlight just how unusual his achievements were, and why, as a result, it is easy to understand and have some sympathy for the Military Police.

***

Henry was also one of the 100 VC recipients selected to form the guard of honour at the funeral of the Unknown Warrior in Westminster Abbey on 11 November 1920.

The idea of commemorating, through burial, an unknown warrior, who could have been a soldier, airman or sailor, and whose body was lying in an unmarked grave, had been put forward earlier in 1920 by the Reverend David Railton, who had served as a chaplain on the Western Front. It is now generally accepted that on the night of 7/8 November 1920, between four and six bodies were exhumed, one from each of the battlefields of Aisne, Somme, Arras and Ypres, and brought to the chapel at St Pol. The bodies were identically covered, and later that night Brigadier General L.J. Wyatt DSO, General Officer Commanding British Troops in France and Flanders, entered the chapel and selected one at random. As a result, the body could not only be from any of the three services, but could come from any part of Britain, its dominions or colonies. It is possible that the body could be that of an unknown warrior from one of Britain's allies. The bodies not selected were re-buried.

The body was then placed in a plain, sealed coffin and, following a church service, it began its journey back to Britain under escort to Boulogne. Whilst there, the coffin was placed inside another made of oak, taken from a tree from the grounds of Hampton Court Palace, and was carried by HMS *Verdun* to Dover, and from there by rail to Victoria station, London, arriving at 8.32 p.m. on 10 November, where it lay overnight at Platform 8. This event is marked by a plaque, which is fixed to the wall adjacent to the railings at the end of that platform (plate 10).

The morning of 11 November saw the coffin begin the final leg of its journey to Westminster Abbey on a gun carriage drawn by six black horses. The pavements were lined with people, many of whom would have seen Henry, as part of the guard of honour, marching past earlier. On the way to the abbey the gun carriage stopped in Whitehall, where George V unveiled the Cenotaph and placed a wreath of red roses and bay leaves on the coffin. The gun carriage then continued on its way to the abbey, accompanied by a group of illustrious pall bearers that included Lord Haig, and was followed by the King. The coffin entered the abbey via the west end of the nave, passing through the guard of honour. After a short service, the King stepped forward and sprinkled French soil on the coffin as it was lowered into the ground. The grave was covered by a silk funeral pall and guarded as thousands of the public filed past to pay their respects. In the week following the burial some 1.25 million people visited the abbey to pay their respects.

★★★

The grave was closed on 18 November and covered by a temporary stone, which had the following inscription on it:

A British Warrior Who Fell In The Great War 1914–1918 For King
And Country. Greater Love Hath No Man Than This.

The black marble stone which covers the grave today was put in place and uncovered at a special service on 11 November 1921. The following inscription is on the marble slab:

Beneath This Stone Rests The Body
Of A British Warrior
Unknown By Name Or Rank
Brought From France To Lie Among
The Most Illustrious Of The Land
And Buried Here On Armistice Day
11 Nov: 1920, In The Presence Of
His Majesty King George V
His Ministers Of State
The Chiefs Of His Forces
And A Vast Concourse Of The Nation
Thus Are Commemorated The Many
Multitudes Who During The Great
War Of 1914–1918 Gave The Most That
Man Can Give Life Itself
For God
For King And Country
For Loved Ones Home And Empire
For The Sacred Cause Of Justice And

The Freedom Of The World
They Buried Him Among The Kings Because He
Had Done Good Toward God And Toward
His House.

★★★

When the Armistice halted the fighting, the division was on high ground east of Havay. After the Great War, Henry was posted to Gibraltar (11 April 1922 to 18 February 1923), Turkey (19 February 1923 to 23 August 1923) and Egypt (24 August 1923 to 29 September 1925). Henry was with the 2nd Battalion in Ireland when he was promoted to lance corporal on 4 February 1921, but he reverted to private at his own request on 8 February 1921, for reasons that are now unknown. He was finally discharged from the army on 5 January 1926, with the rank of sergeant, having served in a recruitment role during his final years in the army. As a VC holder, Henry would return to civilian life with a tax-free government grant of £100 per annum.

For a soldier like Henry, with his long and distinguished service, it seems insensitive and sad, although almost certainly bureaucratically accurate, that his discharge was recorded by the military as being because his 'services were no longer required'. Henry's discharge book describes him as being a model soldier who was very brave, but warned that he needed to control his drinking. The family are dismayed by the comment about Henry and his drinking, and attribute it to nothing more than snobbery and the need on the part of the officers concerned to say something negative to put down this ordinary man.

It is hard to imagine what Henry felt on reading those words but he probably shrugged it off with a rueful smile, prepared to move on to the next stage of his life – a civilian job and marriage.

4

Return to Civilian Life

The year 1926 was to be one of change for Henry on a number of fronts as he left the army, married, moved to Coventry and started a new job. These changes cannot be underestimated, as for sixteen years he had been a soldier where much of his thinking would have been done for him and the necessities of life would have been provided, albeit under a range of different circumstances. Civilian life would be a challenge for him.

In January, Henry was discharged from the army and returned to Leamington Spa, where he married Edith (known as Edie) Warwick in December of that year. Sadly, nothing is known of their courtship or how they met. Eight years after the war had ended, available men were still in short supply because of the huge numbers killed and wounded in that conflict. Henry, therefore, would have had a wider choice where choosing a future spouse was concerned, than would have been the case for Edith. Edith would have thought herself lucky to be marrying Henry, a war hero with the security of a job. Unfortunately for Henry he seemed to not know the type of woman that Edith was to become, as will be discussed later.

Henry then spent the next thirty-eight years working as a commissionaire for the Triumph Motor Company, retiring in 1967 at the age of 76. Henry, as with many ex-servicemen, would have been ideally suited to the position of a commissionaire due to his army background. He was a man who understood the requirements of appearing smartly turned out, because, in effect, when at work he was always going to be on parade. He would also have understood the requirements of guarding facilities for long periods when not very much happened, so, in short, Henry would have known how to conduct himself.

Colleagues remembered him as being quiet, unassuming, modest and deferential, but with his medal ribbons displayed, which added a splash of colour to his dark-blue uniform. In the 1930s, Henry worked in an office in Priory Street, close to Coventry Cathedral. During his long career with the Triumph Motor Company, Henry worked on a number of different sites, including one at Stoke in Coventry.

★★★

The Triumph Motor Company had been founded in 1885 in London but a site was purchased in Much Park Street, Coventry, in 1888 for the manufacture of bicycles. In 1902 the company produced its first motorcycle, and during the Great War it supplied the Allies with 30,000 'Trusty Triumph' motorcycles.

The company was enjoying success and in 1920 purchased the former Hillman car factory in Coventry, producing its first car in 1923 under the name Triumph Motor Company. Following bankruptcy in 1939, the company was purchased by T. W. Ward at a time when the Second World War brought an end to the production of cars. The company reverted to the production of motorcycles, and in 1940 some 40,000 were supplied to the Allies.

In 1944, the company was purchased by the Standard Motor Company, which made the decision in 1950 to use the Standard name on saloon cars and the Triumph name on sports cars. The final change of ownership happened in 1960, when Leyland Motors took over, with the final Triumph being produced in 1981. Although the iconic name of Triumph has now disappeared from motorcars, the trademark is owned by BMW, and Triumph motorcycles are still produced.

The period 1926 to 1967 was a time of much change at the company, throughout which Henry was there in his commissionaire's uniform. The 1960s were also a troubled period for the British motor industry as it was beset with strikes, layoffs and a downturn caused by a credit squeeze. The Standard Triumph Motor Company was not immune from this, and extracts from *The Times* newspaper shed some light on this by detailing the events of 1960, as outlined below.

The Standard Triumph International Group had taken over Mulliners Limited in October 1959, and on 31 January 1960 there was a strike by members of the National Union of Vehicle Builders who were employed at Mulliners. As a result, 2,000 workers at Standard Triumph were laid off indefinitely, and if the strike had continued the same outcome would have affected all of its 11,000 workers.

Tensions and tempers were bound to have run high and Henry would have been very much to the fore, ensuring that security at the company's premises was maintained. On 1 February, a further 4,000 workers were laid off but, thankfully, for all concerned the strike at Mulliners ended on 2 February, and by the following day production returned to normal. A second strike at Mulliners started on 9 February and this did not end until the 22nd, by which time car production had once again been affected.

On 14 March, at the instigation of the Standard Triumph Motor Company, all 150 workers at Mulliners were sacked without notice. There was an inevitable backlash from its own 11,000 workers, who refused to handle vehicle parts that Mulliners workers had produced and there was a ban on overtime. The company had to moderate its position and on 15 March it offered to find jobs for those men sacked by Mulliners. Finally, on 24 March, a shorter working week was introduced for all 11,000 employees.

These were troubled times, and Henry would have experienced a different form of conflict. Where did his sympathies lie? This question cannot be answered, but if Henry was of a socialist persuasion then his sympathies would have been for the men laid off. Alternatively, this may have been a world that he would still have regarded quizzically, following his army service where an officer's word was law, when he saw unions and men defying their management.

★★★

Henry and Edith moved from Leamington Spa to Coventry, due to Henry's job with Triumph. They first settled at 22 Cope Street, now the site of the Coventry Sports Centre, and from here Henry was able to travel to his workplace while Edith worked on her needlework. Edith, a petite and somewhat precious woman, described herself as a needle-work professional, and the Tandey family recall stories that she may have produced some fine embroidery for unspecified members of the Royal Family. Taking the view that her hands were her livelihood, Edith refused to carry shopping or undertake housework, in order to protect them. She is remembered within the Tandey family as being domineering and rude, and therefore was somewhat of an unpopular figure. Consequently, on top of his work, it fell to Henry to keep the home going by doing the housework and the cooking.

Along with many other homes and businesses, 22 Cope Street was destroyed by the German bombing on 14 November 1940. Although Henry, then an ARP warden, showed great bravery during that night in saving people from their damaged homes, he could not save his and Edith's first home in Coventry. Fortunately, at the time of the bombing, Edith was staying with her sister in Leamington Spa, or Henry's loss may have been greater than bricks, mortar and possessions.

★★★

It was in August 1938 that Henry first learned that he had been identified by Adolf Hitler as the soldier who had spared his life on 28 September 1918 at Marcoing. The story of how Henry was informed of Hitler's claim is almost as interesting as the claim itself and will be discussed in Chapter 5.

The outbreak of the Second World War saw Henry try to re-enlist; he still saw himself as a soldier and felt that he wanted to do his bit, and maybe he was also motivated by a feeling that if he had spared Hitler's life then he had a responsibility to try to put matters right. Henry was not deemed fit enough to enlist due to the wounds he had received in the First World War, including the loss of a toe. Probably with his tongue firmly planted in his cheek, a reporter asked Henry about this, to which he replied, '... but I might try for a gunner in the Air Force if they'll have me.' Nevertheless, Henry still carried a cachet as a war hero and he was given, for the duration of the war only, the honorary rank of sergeant while engaged in recruiting duties.

★★★

Edith died of a stroke in 1958, and in March 1963 Henry remarried, living the remainder of his life at 7 Loudon Road, Radford in Coventry. Henry's second wife was Annie Whateley, who had been born in Germany in about 1921 with the family name Kietzmann, and she was to prove another woman who was a strong character and unpopular with his family. Unsurprisingly for a German of her age, Annie had been a member of the Hitler Youth in Munich, which certainly did not endear her to the family.

Annie had become known to Henry when Harry Whateley (1916–99) returned with her from Germany at the end of the Second World War and introduced her to his family, and also to the Tandeys. It is open to speculation as to exactly how much of a welcome Annie received from the Whateleys, because they would have had to have been unusually forgiving to have accepted her, with her German heritage, following the Second World War.

Harry Whateley must have been aware of the strong anti-German feelings, particularly in Coventry just eight years after the city had been bombed, and must have anticipated the likely reaction of his family. Nevertheless, the marriage went ahead at Coventry Register Office on 21 August 1948. It was not a happy marriage and the couple were divorced by 1953, with Annie sometime later going to live with Henry and Edith as a lodger. It is true to say that no one on the Tandey side of the family have anything good to say about either of Henry's wives, and they smile when contemplating the thought of these two particular women living cheek by jowl and periodically falling out.

The British were to harbour resentment and hostility to the Germans long after the war ended in 1945. Annie's integration would not have been made easier by the fact that she spoke in broken English with a heavy German accent, and she was described as quite a fierce woman with an alleged alcohol problem. In fairness to Annie her grasp of English, coupled with her accent, may have made her seem curt and abrupt.

Henry would have been aware of the anti-German sentiments that abounded at the time of Annie's first marriage, and they would still have been present in 1963. To add another ingredient to the mix, the Tandeys were a Roman Catholic family, so a further issue for them, where Annie was concerned, was the fact that she was a divorcee.

Despite any such feelings, and any insight Henry had gained as to her character through her years of living with him as a lodger, they nevertheless married, but whether this was the result of love or a mutual need for companionship is not possible to say. Annie would have been aware of Henry's situation and his fame as a VC holder, and, perhaps, was aware that he was careful with his money, with some put away, so it is possible that she took the initiative and pressed for them to get married.

Where Henry was concerned, it is likely that Annie had started to help around the house, particularly after Edith's death, and so, as unromantic as it sounds, this may well have been a marriage of convenience for both of them. Henry had probably, despite her character failings, got used to having Annie around and agreed to the marriage, perhaps eager not to lose whatever level of companionship she offered. Henry, who had displayed such bravery in battle, maybe felt unable or unwilling to stand firm against strong and perhaps unpleasant women, ending up marrying two of them. Both women are remembered by those on the Tandey side of the family as 'monsters'.

Within the family, Annie is remembered as never being particularly warm or loving towards Henry, and was constantly nagging and criticising him, acting more as a carer than a wife. Another factor in this marriage was the large age gap between them as Henry was 72 and Annie was in her early forties. At times she was heard to refer to him as a 'silly old man' and although Henry resented this, he was never seen or heard to retaliate.

Annie often accompanied Henry to events in London, where she is remembered for being loud and arrogant. She liked to wear expensive clothes and jewellery, accompanied by a very heavy perfume, which could have been used to mask the effect of her chain smoking habit. The Tandeys would stay, while in London, with Henry's brother George. Annie is remembered as enjoying their visits to London, in particular the Buckingham Palace garden parties, despite often voicing her dislike of her adopted country.

Although Annie is not remembered by the family in a particularly favourable light, she was highly practical and hard working around the home, and is remembered for her ability to paint and decorate the house virtually overnight. There was, though, no real warmth between Henry and Annie, who appeared almost to live separate lives, with Henry going to bed early, usually by 9 p.m., with a book and Annie regularly going out with her friends. It seems that Annie enjoyed drinking and gambling, and in particular enjoyed playing on the slot machines and bingo. For the other members of the Tandey family, Annie was viewed as an oddity on the few occasions when they met.

Henry Gordon remembers Henry as being a generous man willing to provide a bed and a bath to those who were in need and would always help his family financially. He is remembered as a perfectionist in all that he did, but, strangely, is not remembered as having any hobbies or pastimes; despite his interest in sport as a youth, he had none in it after he left the army, either as a participant or a spectator.

The family also remember Henry as a normal man who never spoke about his war exploits, as someone who possessed a good sense of humour, with an answer for everything, and was prone to singing 'I'm 'enery the Eighth I am', a popular music hall song.

Sadly, there is evidence that towards the end of his life Henry was not a particularly happy man as his health declined. Perhaps his second marriage was also a factor, as it was described by the family as 'a rotten marriage'. When, towards the end of his life, Henry was asked to complete a questionnaire for his local British Legion branch he 'crossed through the bit about date of marriage, wife's name, and family', leaving the branch's representative to comment that he was 'either a confirmed bachelor or just a married man who valued his privacy'. There was perhaps another explanation, namely that he had stopped viewing his and Annie's situation as a marriage.

★★★

On 23 July 1957, Canon W.M. Lummis wrote to Henry via the Regimental Association of the Duke of Wellington's Regiment. Canon Lummis had, from an early age, had an interest in the VC holders, and his hobby, which he maintained as an adult, was to create a file of information on each of them. These are known as the Lummis Files and are now kept in the Templer Study Centre at the National Army Museum in London.

Canon Lummis wrote to Henry seeking to clear up the confusion around Henry having two regimental numbers, namely 34506 in the 5th Battalion of the Duke of Wellington's Regiment, and 9545 in the 5th Battalion of the Green Howards, posing the question as to whether he had ever been in the two regiments, or had been attached to only one of them. Lummis asked Henry to supply his dates of enlistment and demobilisation, any other interesting information, and, if possible, a photograph, adding that Henry's file required a good deal of additional particulars. At the end of his letter Lummis comments that he had not had the opportunity of meeting Henry at the previous year's centenary commemoration when he, Lummis, had been present at the review, the abbey service, the exhibition and the Guildhall reception.

Lummis' letter was forwarded to Henry, who replied on 16 August 1957. The letter is very formal and sets out the facts of Henry's life but with few glimpses of the man behind them. In response to the request for a photograph, Henry writes simply, 'Sorry, I cannot supply you with a photo & don't possess one'. Henry may not personally have had any photographs as a result of his home being destroyed in the bombing of Coventry in 1940, but photographs were in the possession of family members, as they still are, but Henry clearly did not feel inclined, for whatever reason, to approach them.

Henry was proud of the fact that he had never accepted promotion and in his reply to Lummis made the point, writing:

> For your records: I went through the 1914–1918 War refusing promotion gaining all honours as a private soldier.

There is no comment in Henry's letter about the commemoration event referred to in Lummis' letter, and no engagement in a more social way – his reply was brief and to the point.

Lummis replied to Henry on 27 August 1957, thanking him for the information he had supplied. Henry had, it transpired, sent Lummis copies of the citations for each of his awards. Lummis returned these with the comment:

> The citations for each of your decorations prove that you well deserved each of them, and, in particular, the Victoria Cross. The citation in the Divisional Order is, of course, very much fuller than that which appeared in the London Gazette. These I return as you may like them back. I have taken copies of them.

Canon Lummis reveals in this letter that he had served in the Marcoing area shortly before Henry won his VC:

On the day that you were at Marcoing my regiment, The Suffolk Regiment, in the 3rd Division, was in reserve there. However, I was not with them just then having gone home on leave immediately after we had crossed the Canal du Nord and taken Flesquieres on September 26th. I got my company over the Canal under shell and machine gun fire just as the barrage started, having only one subaltern who had only come out quite fresh to warfare from England a few days before. I recommended my Coy-Sergt-Major for a DCM for his gallant work in getting the company over; but he was only awarded a third bar to his MM. Lord Gort further up the Canal, was awarded the VC for similar services.

This comment reveals a number of things. Firstly, Lummis had knowledge of the scene of Henry's display of exceptional bravery, and secondly, that he wanted to share with Henry that he too had seen action. Thirdly, it is clear that it still rankled Lummis many, many years later that his company sergeant major was not awarded the DCM, while Lord Gort received the VC for 'similar services'. This last point shows the unfairness many servicemen felt in the distribution of the bravery awards, as there was an element of chance involved, in that it was possible for two soldiers operating in different parts of the line, and displaying similar levels of courage or bravery to receive different levels of award, or, indeed, no award at all. It might also show that officers were more inclined to receive the higher awards than other ranks.

It would be interesting to know what Henry made of that comment, as almost certainly he would have had a view after his service on the Western Front. In any event, Henry's reply did not reveal a desire to share reminiscences with Lummis.

★★★

Henry's reply to Lummis was in keeping with his being a private man, as was described in the *Leamington Courier* (15 March 1974):

It is only with reluctance that he talks about himself – a modest attitude which has always typified him.

He seemed, though, to enjoy attending the regimental reunions where he could be among old comrades. Henry relished attending these events but also saw it as an obligation to those who the war had prevented from ever attending such occasions.

Henry was a proud and active member of the Old Contemptibles' Association, which had been formed in 1925, with 178 British branches and fourteen overseas. Members of the association were known as 'chums', and they were all survivors of the 1914 British Expeditionary Force that took on the advancing German Army between August and November 1914 to keep it from capturing the Channel ports. The name of the association is taken from the order from Kaiser Wilhelm II to his men to 'walk over General French's contemptible little army'. The last member of the association died in 2005.

In August 1933, Henry set off with seven others to attend the Old Contemptibles' Association's annual church service at Burton parish church. The Coventry contingent travelled in four cars, and between Nuneaton and Burton one of the vehicles, in which Henry was a passenger, was involved in an accident. Without warning, two cyclists came out of a narrow lane into the middle of the road and, in attempting to avoid them, the car had to swerve on to a grass verge, where unfortunately a party of picnickers were gathered by the side of a stationary car. In order to avoid the picnickers, the driver had no alternative but to pull back on to the road, whereupon the car overturned. Two members of the party were injured and required medical assistance, and a third person who was injured was due to bear the flag of the Coventry branch at the service. But Old Contemptibles were made of stern stuff, and, having got help for the injured the rest of the party, continued to Burton in the remaining three vehicles. What of the injured, old soldier, who was due to carry the flag? He declined immediate medical help, continued to Burton, and paraded with the flag as he had been designated to do.

The Old Contemptibles' Association played an important part in Henry's life. In August 1933, there was an annual parade at Horse Guards Parade in London, which some 2,000 members marched from Wellington Barracks led by the band of the Grenadier Guards. The ceremony involved the laying of a wreath, which was carried by Henry, Colonel C.C. Frost and Mr J. Upton.

One of the founder members of the association's Coventry branch was Charles Gregory, who died suddenly in May 1935. The funeral took place at the Windmill Road Cemetery in Foleshill, Coventry, where it was well attended, with Henry as one of the six pall bearers.

In 1932, Henry and the two other VC holders from Leamington Spa attended a Sacred Concert of Remembrance at the town's Theatre Royal, and on 22 March 1935, he attended an exhibition of war films and watched a film entitled *Forgotten Man* at the Coventry Empire Theatre.

However, not all the events that Henry attended were of a serious nature, and in April 1935 he and a representative party of the Old Contemptibles met the original Mademoiselle from Armentieres, Mrs A.E. Rogers. Mrs Rogers had been only 15½ years old at the outbreak of the war but she and the old soldiers recalled her cooking *pomme frites* and *des oeufs*, as well as the humour of her attempts to speak English and their attempts to speak French.

On a more serious note, the *Daily Express* reported on 10 March 1939 that Henry had started a scheme to help the rank-and-file VC holders who, as a result of age or infirmity, could not earn a living. Through the article he asked for those wanting to help or for those affected to contact him at his address in Cope Street. Sadly, no further information is available as to how successful this initiative proved and what was achieved.

★★★

The *Daily Telegraph* reported on 27 September 1963, under the headline 'VC Going for Beer and Songs', about a Green Howards reunion that Henry was to attend at the Queen Elizabeth Barracks, at Strensall, near York. Henry was one of 400 attendees, of which 100 were to be Great War veterans. The organisers had arranged for a trench, which they hoped would seem authentic, to be dug on waste ground at the barracks for Henry and the others to visit. The trench acted as a catalyst for conversation based on their shared, but positive, memories and experiences, as tends to be the case when old soldiers get together. The reunion was, the organisers said, to be about beer, bangers and mouth organ music. Judging by the photograph (plate 15), Henry and his comrades looked to be enjoying themselves, with some wearing helmets, music playing and a drink or two being appreciated.

Henry recognised that the reunions started to lose their purpose the more that he and others attended them, but the reunion described above seems to have been special because he felt that sitting in a trench again and talking over the old days had brought back a flood of memories. For Henry, that reunion had proved to be more meaningful for those attending than perhaps those organising it had anticipated.

The *Green Howards Gazette*, spring 1978 issue, carried Henry's obituary and commented that he had enjoyed attending reunions where he 'thoroughly enjoyed what he called a "tiddly" or two'. Henry's family remember him as a sober man, partial to the odd half of Bass, except for when he was with his old comrades. He would sometimes take his nephew, Henry Gordon, or his brother, George, to some of the reunions in London, but always made a point, as a precaution, of telling them which train he had to catch from Euston back to Coventry so that they could ensure that he caught it! Henry was quite adamant that this was part and parcel of them being his host when he was their guest, and that it fell to them to look after him in all respects.

Henry was invited to attend a regimental reunion on 20–21 September 1969, which, again, was to be held at the barracks at Strensall, but replied that he was not able to attend due to arthritis. Arthritis was becoming a problem for Henry; he again turned down an invitation to attend the 1972 reunion saying that, 'He could not get far on two sticks'. Happily, his arthritis had improved enough so that when the Green Howards Regimental Museum was opened on 25 July 1973, he was able to travel to Richmond for the opening, where he was presented to His Majesty King Olav V of Norway, who was, at that time, the colonel-in-chief.

Henry was a regular guest at Victoria Cross and George Cross meetings, and took part in a commemoration parade for the sixtieth anniversary of the Battle of the Somme in Leamington Spa, held on 1 July 1976. He was the guest of honour, taking the salute outside the town hall just sixteen months before he died, and at a time when he was seriously affected by arthritis. His attendance produced a headline in a local paper, the *Coventry Evening Telegraph* (2 July 1976): 'VC Hero at Parade to Mark Battle of Somme.' The article referred to Henry as 'Leamington's most famous soldier on parade yesterday'. When asked what he had thought of the occasion, Henry is reported to have replied that 'The parade was very good'.

Although he was a proud veteran, Henry was a modest man who wanted to go about his life without fuss or bother, and his attitude is summed up when he said (*Leamington Spa Courier*):

> After the Victoria Cross they tried to make me into a glamour boy, but I wouldn't have that. Soldiers aren't glamour boys.

Henry mistrusted the newspapers almost certainly after his brushes with them over the story that he had spared Adolf Hitler's life. He wrote a letter in May 1974 to Mr A.V. Simpson, who had also served in the 5th Battalion of the Duke of Wellington's, although it is not clear whether this was in the Great War, thanking him for having corrected some misrepresentation about him in a local paper. Henry wrote:

> I spent a few days in London last week … my brother handed me a cutting from the Leamington paper where you put them right about me. I never bother about it, the papers seem to get everything wrong … the reason I don't entertain reporters, they get nothing from me.

There is some evidence that Henry was a man who could harbour resentments, which, perhaps, was a trait passed on by his father. Henry, as was discussed earlier, appeared to resent the lack of opportunities for recognition with the Green Howards, and also talked about the jealousy he felt he had experienced from his fellow soldiers after he had received his gallantry medals. In this particular instance, Henry may well have continued to resent the way the press had reacted to what he had said in 1940, and the attention that this had caused to someone who was described by family members as a very private man who liked to enjoy a quiet life.

Although Henry enjoyed attending reunions, and other events in London and elsewhere, he felt, at times, that no one paid him any attention or spoke to him. He wrote of this to Mr A.V. Simpson on 12 June 1972, following his attendance at a Duke of Wellington's reunion, where he had not met anyone from the 5th Battalion:

> Many thanks for letter. Nice to hear from someone of the 5th Battalion of the Dukes. I have been to Halifax and Huddersfield many times to reunions but I have met none of the 5th.
>
> I have tried to get the history of the 5th, no-one seems to have wrote anything about them.

In a further letter to Simpson on 28 May 1974, he made a further comment about these reunions:

> I did not serve very long and no-one ever came up to speak to me about the 5th Battalion at the dinners.

It is quite understandable that by 1974, veterans from the 5th Battalion, who had served with Henry during those few short weeks in 1918, might be few and far between. Nevertheless, it seems sad that he felt ignored as it is easy to imagine Henry sitting there with his medal ribbons on his chest, one of which was for the VC, feeling excluded. By 1974 it is quite possible, and perhaps understandable, that not everyone attending would have known who he was and what he had achieved.

★★★

The 1970s saw Henry's health and mobility start to seriously decline. Amongst the papers of the Cridlan family, owners of the Regent Hotel, held at the Warwickshire Archives, there are some letters that confirm Henry was suffering badly from arthritis. On 6 February 1981, F.J. Cridlan wrote a letter to Mr A. V. Simpson, in which he says we 'last spoke some two years before he died. He was very crippled.'

In his 1972 letter to Simpson, Henry had written about his increasing infirmity, citing arthritis as the cause. He went on to say:

> If you do manage to get down this way we shall have quite a lot to talk about. I cannot get far, I get around a bit with two sticks. Please let me know if you do get this way as I sometimes get a run around by car by some of my friends.

In 1976 Henry became seriously ill and in December of that year he was admitted to the Walsgrave Hospital, in Coventry, with rectal bleeding. It was clear to the doctors that he had a malignant growth in his rectum that could only be dealt with by surgery. This would be serious surgery for anyone, but Henry was now aged 85 and, given his age, his service and wounds from the Great War, he was a relatively frail man. The medical staff found him a little depressed and unsure of whether or not he wanted the operation to proceed, but he was nevertheless pleasant and courteous to deal with.

Henry was befriended by the senior registrar, Mr Michael Crumplin, who spent time both before and after his operation, talking to him, and eventually got him to speak about his army life. Henry gradually started to talk about his Great War experiences as he came to realise that Mr Crumplin, whose father had also served in the Great War, was genuinely interested, rather than just being polite. At no time, however, did Henry talk about the incident with Hitler and Mr Crumplin only read of this in later articles and obituaries.

Henry responded to this gentle counselling, and accepted from Mr Crumplin that there was no alternative to surgery, so he agreed that the operation could go ahead. The operation was performed by Mr Crumplin, and it involved serious invasive surgery, which left Henry with a colostomy bag. Medical treatment and expertise has advanced since 1976, and a patient facing the same operation today may well be able to have the two ends of the bowel reconnected once the cancer had been removed. But today, even if a colostomy is still necessary, there are now stoma nurses to support patients, and many more products that individuals can use to manage their situation – none of which was available to Henry at the time of his surgery.

Remarkably, Mr Crumplin has no recollection of meeting Annie Tandey, or of discussing Henry's condition, the proposed treatment, prognosis or his aftercare with her or any other member of the family. Given Henry's age and the seriousness of his situation this seems to portray a cold and uncaring attitude on the part of his relatives, in particular Annie, who would have been expected to visit, despite her husband's desire, mentioned below, to have no visitors.

A note in a file of papers held at the Green Howards Museum, made after Henry had undergone the operation, revealed the seriousness of Henry's condition, as conveyed by the following comment: 'I think at his age he will have a fight on his hands to win.'

On 6 December, he was visited by Major Derek Outhwaite who set out how he found him in a two-person bay in Ward B2:

> I have been along to Harry Tandey and considering his age he is coming through pretty well. The hospital is a fine modern one, and he is on a small 2 bed ward.
>
> The old boy is a very independent type and says he is being well looked after and wants nothing – not even visitors. Gwen and I are going along to see his wife and she will probably tell us if we can really help.

It was while Henry was in his post-operative recovery stage that he agreed to ask Annie to bring in his medals, and Mr Crumplin took a photograph of him holding them while he sat on the side of his bed (plate 21). Henry was described by his doctor as a good patient, and he recovered sufficiently to return home on 13 December.

On leaving hospital he was again visited by Major Outhwaite and his wife Gwen, who commented in a further letter about how they found him 'in very good fettle and more lively and talkative than he was in hospital', and ended by saying, 'I took the old boy along some scotch'. The Regimental Association reimbursed the major for the £10 cost of the scotch by cheque on 20 December.

★★★

Henry, now aged 86, was not to escape the cancer and died at home from carcinoma of the rectum in the early hours of 20 December 1977. Henry's death certificate (entry number 247) shows that Annie was present at his death and is recorded as the informant. During this final stage of his life, Henry was regularly visited by his GP, Dr John Maclean, who was 88 at the time of writing this book and sadly unable to remember this patient.

Henry was entitled to a full military funeral but that was not what he wanted. Accordingly, his was to be a private funeral, and at Henry's request people were asked not to send flowers but to make a donation instead to the Scanner Appeal Fund for the Walsgrave Hospital in Coventry.

His funeral took place on 23 December and the arrangements were made through the undertakers Pargetter and Son of Coventry by Annie, his brother, George, and sister, Magdeline. Henry's body was conveyed to the Church of Christ the King, in an elm-veneered coffin, for an early morning service conducted by Father Michael McTernan, followed by cremation at 10.40 a.m. at the Canley Crematorium in Coventry.

Despite Henry's wishes, he was provided with a guard of honour by nine members of the Triumph Motor Branch of the Royal British Legion, who came with a wreath with the letters VC picked out in flowers. The Coventry No. 4 (Triumph Motors) Branch of the Royal British Legion had been founded in 1934, and it is believed that Henry was one of the founder members. The branch still meets on the second Tuesday of every month at the Standard Triumph Social Club in Tile Hill, Coventry.

Both the mayors of Coventry and Royal Leamington Spa were also in attendance.

Henry's death produced a number of tributes and newspaper headlines, such as 'Coventry War Hero Dies at 86' (*Coventry Evening Telegraph*, 20 December 1977), and 'A Last Tribute to Valour' (*Coventry Evening Telegraph*, 23 December 1977).

However, he was still unable to escape his name being again linked to that of Hitler: 'Hitler's "Captor" Dies' (*Daily Telegraph*, 22 December 1977).

★★★

Henry had stated his wish that his ashes should be scattered at Marcoing, but this was not possible for both practical and legal reasons, and he was made aware of this. In a letter dated 7 September 1971 from Colonel Forbes of the Green Howards to a Mrs A. W. Thompson, the practical reasons are outlined:

> Henry Tandey wanted his ashes scattered at the Petit Kruiseke crossroads
> – crossroads is today at the centre of a busy thoroughfare with traffic
> lights therefore inappropriate to be scattered there.

Henry would probably have been unaware, and may well have been surprised, that the site he had fought over was now in the centre of a built-up area.

Legally, the French would not allow his ashes to be scattered and so his ashes were buried, but without any form of ceremony, close to another VC winner in the British Cemetery at Masnières in October 1978. Henry's friend, Mr Clive Bacon, helped with these arrangements and liaised with the War Graves Commission together with the undertakers, Pargetter and Son. The casket containing Henry's ashes had to be taken to the French Embassy by the undertakers for official sealing in the presence of a French official. Pargetter and Son also had to liaise with the mayor and the head of police for the Masnières/Marcoing area to ensure that the necessary papers to allow the internment were issued.

In a letter dated 17 January 1978, Mrs B. Walton, Director General of the War Graves Commission, set out the legal position in a letter to Colonel Forbes:

> Unfortunately under French Law, the scattering of ashes is not permitted but it is possible to have the casket containing the ashes of Mr Tandey interred in a cemetery in France ... not possible for any form of commemoration to be made in memory of Mr Tandey.

Mrs Walton recommended the Masnières British Cemetery at Marcoing, which contained the graves of several members of the Duke of Wellington's Regiment who had lost their lives in the September 1918 action. Had Henry's family still wanted his ashes to be scattered then they were asked to consider Brookwood Military Cemetery in Woking, Surrey.

It seems a sad and callous way for the ashes of a true hero to be treated, and this is a point made in a letter from the Regimental Secretary of the Duke of Wellington's to Henry's brother, George, on 25 April 1978:

> It did seem a little 'callous' for his ashes to be taken to France and simply placed in the ground without any ceremony however simple, nor representation from the regiments he served in.

Henry's ashes were collected by his nephew, Henry Gordon, the son of Henry's sister, Magdeline, on 13 May 1978, who, accompanied by his son Tony Gordon, took them to France for the internment. Annie Tandey, perhaps as a further indication of her relationship with her late husband, did not attend, having indicated her intention not to attend as far back as January. Henry and Tony Gordon waited, on what was a sunny day, until the French cemetery attendant arrived on his bicycle to dig the hole into which the casket was to be interred. And, in accordance with French procedure, there was no commemoration or ceremonial allowed which, according to the War Graves Commission, formed part of the conditions laid down by the French for permitting the British to lease the land for the cemetery.

Henry Gordon wrote to Pargetter and Son on 23 May 1978 to say that the ashes had been interred and that 'the job had been done in a quiet and dignified manner'.

On 3 January 1978, Colonel Forbes wrote to Annie Tandey to express his condolences, during which he made clear the esteem in which Henry was held, saying:

> I am writing to offer you my personal deep sympathy to you for your very great loss. After sharing your life for so long with a man like Henry (Harry?), you are bound to miss him a great deal.
>
> In the regiment he was almost a legend.
>
> I know that he will always be remembered by the Regiment as a very special sort of man.

The Green Howards had decided to send a VC plate to the families of each of the regiment's eighteen recipients, and Annie Tandey was duly sent her plate on 13 July 1979. The whereabouts of this plate today are not known.

In 1978, the Royal Borough of Leamington Spa had a maple tree planted in Henry's memory in the town's Jephson Gardens, in response to an approach by Henry's friend Clive Bacon. The chair of the town's Recreation and Amenities Committee, Councillor Norman Parker, described it as 'an excellent idea' and the tree was planted by Annie in the presence of friends, family, and the mayors of Leamington and Warwick. Unfortunately, for those visiting the gardens today the plaque has now disappeared and the significance of the tree concerned has been lost. Warwick District Council also named a development 'Henry Tandey Court' in Leamington Spa after him.

★★★

On 26 November 1980, Annie sold Henry's medals to a private collector. The circumstances surrounding this are interesting, as Henry had donated his medals to the Duke of Wellington's Regimental Museum in 1960, perhaps unsurprisingly as this was the regiment he was serving in at the time he was awarded his gallantry medals. The accession, or formal donation, is recorded in the museum's records under entry number 1960.1, and although, sadly, the actual date was not included, it must have been very early in the year due to the entry number. By this generous action, Henry's medals legally became the property of the trustees of the Duke of Wellington's Regiment.

Later that year, Henry borrowed the medals back to wear at an Armistice Day event, but he never returned them. It is open to question as to why Henry did not return the medals. Even though the Duke of Wellington's Regiment chose not to chase him for the medals' return, Henry must have known that this was something that he should have done. It had to be a conscious decision on Henry's part to retain the medals, and therefore stands as an episode of his life where his actions can be criticised.

A rumour that has been passed down the regiment through the years is that Henry occasionally used the medals, when they were in his possession, to pawn them for alcohol. Henry's family are adamant that he was firstly not a man who needed to pawn anything, and secondly that he was not heavy drinker. The rumour echoes a comment on Henry's discharge papers about his need to control his drinking, but his family view this as nothing more than snobbery and an attempt to put him in his place.

Alternatively, an article in the magazine *Iron Duke*, the regimental magazine for the Duke of Wellington's, speculated that the medals were not returned because Henry had learnt of their potential monetary value and had decided to hold on to them as an 'inheritance' for his family because, as will be discussed later, he made a will leaving everything to his wife Annie. Henry Gordon is adamant that his uncle would not have wanted his medals to have been sold.

There are many photographs of Henry at reunions and other events from 1960 through to 1976, where he can be seen proudly wearing his medals, so it is unlikely that he ever considered selling the medals. Before casting Annie in the role of villainess, a legitimate question to ask would be did she know what had transpired in 1960, given that she did not marry Henry until 1963, and therefore naturally assumed that at his death the medals would pass to her? It is quite possible that, without the intervention of any other interested parties, Annie would go on to sell the medals in all good faith.

Shortly before his death, Henry was approached by the Green Howards to complete a questionnaire, which he did somewhat reluctantly. At some point in this process Henry was asked directly whether he would eventually give his medals to the regiment and he wrote in reply:

> I am afraid I shall have to leave my medals with the Leamington Museum as I belong to two regiments.

At the point that he made his will and completed the questionnaire, the medals were not legally Henry's to dispose of – he would have known that they were legally owned by the Duke of Wellington's. The regiment was reluctant to seek the return of the medals from Annie because it was not the 'done thing' to do so, and they particularly did not want to be seen as harassing a VC holder or his family.

According to members of the family, Henry's original will left the medals to the Duke of Wellington's Regimental Museum. Although no date can be attributed to this, it is likely that the will pre-dated the donation of the medals to the Duke of Wellington's. Shortly before he died, Henry made another will in which he left the medals and all his estate to Annie. Two points need to be made; firstly the medals were not Henry's to dispose of, and secondly, the will gave Annie the means to justify her claim on the medals and her later decision to sell them. It seems strange that, if the family knew of Henry's wishes for the disposal of his medals, they apparently chose not to take any action to stop their sale.

In 1980, Annie Tandey decided to put Henry's medals up for auction because she said that she needed the money. It is not clear why Annie felt in need of money because the marital home was paid for; however, it is known that she was a keen gambler, drinker and liked socialising. There is a feeling amongst some family members that Annie felt that either she could not cope, or could not be bothered with Henry's military legacy and so chose to dispose of the medals. In any event, once the medals were sold, Annie had little or no contact with the Tandey side of the family. Whatever her reasons, the medals were legally not her property to dispose of, and the regiment, not wishing to court public disapproval, chose not to exert its own rights over those of Henry's widow for the return of the medals, which remained the legal property of the museum.

The Green Howards were aware of the impending sale and thought they would sell for £10,000. On 5 August 1980, the Regimental Secretary, Lieutenant Colonel Scrope, wrote to Annie Tandey and arranged to visit her for a chat, and planned to take the opportunity to talk to her about the medals, which was confirmed in a second letter sent to Clive Bacon that day. Whatever Annie and her visitor discussed it failed to stop the medals going to auction.

In replying to the letter to Clive Bacon, Lieutenant Colonel Scrope talks about another claimant for the medals:

> I was very interested to hear that Mr Henry Whateley, Tandey's nephew, claims that he should have the medals.

Harry Whateley, the ex-husband of Annie, claimed that she had no legal right to sell Henry's medals. His claim was based on the fact that he was, in his words, the family's oldest soldier, and that Henry had said that he should inherit the medals. On another occasion, he claimed that his relative, Edith Tandey, Henry's first wife who had died in 1958, had told him that, as she and Henry had not had any children, he should be the one to inherit the medals.

At the time of Edith Tandey's death the medals were still the legal property of Henry, so their disposal to a relative or friend was an option, but how likely was it that Harry Whateley would be the one selected? If Henry was aware of Edith's wishes, then it seems that he had no plans to honour them.

Harry Whateley was the black sheep of the family, who never seemed to remain anywhere very long or keep in regular contact with his family; he did, however, keep in contact with his ex-wives. As a result of his continued contact with Annie he was likely to have known that the medals were to be sold at auction and their guide price. While it might be tempting to see Harry Whateley as an honourable individual trying to keep the medals in the family, the truth is that it was more likely to be an opportunistic attempt to hijack Annie's plans, and then, in all likelihood, sell them himself. Family members can recall Harry as a jolly man, and his 'chuntering' on about the medals on the infrequent occasions when they met, but without taking any interest in what he was saying.

The medals were sold at auction by Annie at Sotheby's in November 1980 for what was then a record sum of £27,000, topping a bid of £26,000 made by the Royal Borough of Leamington Spa, which had wanted to buy the medals for the town. To achieve this, the council had brought together a consortium comprising Warwick District Council, the Regent Hotel, a group of Leamington businessmen, and the Victoria and Albert Museum, to be led by Councillor Norman Parker. The consortium felt quietly confident that, as the guide price was £12,000 and the world record price for the sale of a VC was £17,000, their available funds of £25,000 would be sufficient.

Norman Parker, Frank Cridlan and Alan Pedley spent some five hours waiting for Henry's medals to come up for auction. Their sale started, and the consortium found that it was in competition with a lone, and anonymous, bidder, whose hand ominously kept going up. Despite only having £25,000 pledged, Norman Parker went up to £26,000 but felt that he could go no further. He was devastated not to have successfully purchased the medals. He had, in fact, been so confident of winning that he had, somewhat embarrassingly, arranged for the local press to be present.

Neither of Henry's regiments chose to attempt to buy the medals, and in any event the eventual sale price would have been beyond their means.

After the auction, Norman Parker was able to meet briefly with the lone bidder, who turned out to be Sir Ernest Harrison. Norman

Parker started by explaining who he was and what he was trying to do on behalf of Leamington Spa. He asked Sir Ernest whether he would be willing to let him take the medals back to Leamington Spa to be put on display for two weeks. Sir Ernest was agreeable to that but said it could not be for a couple of weeks because he was going to have new ribbons put on the medals. Norman Parker was dismayed by what he saw as nothing less than a cavalier disregard for the significance of the original ribbons, which had been handled by both George V and Henry, but there was nothing he could do to prevent their separation.

Eventually, Norman Parker was told that the medal ribbons had been replaced and he went to London to collect the medals. On arrival he was ushered into a room at the auctioneers where he found that the medals were in a box, inside a paper bag, along with the old ribbons. On seeing a large container filled with discarded medal ribbons, he asked what was going to happen to those from Henry's medals. He was told that they would be thrown away, but fortunately he was asked whether he wanted them and, amazed but extremely pleased to be asked, he said yes immediately.

Norman Parker was pleased to secure the medal ribbons because amongst them was the original VC ribbon and he returned from London with them in a paper bag; he has since had them framed and they now hang on his study wall. The medals themselves, complete with their new ribbons, finally went on display to the public in Leamington Spa Museum and Library in January 1981.

Following the auction of Henry's medals, Norman Parker met with Annie Tandey to explain that his attempt to purchase the medals had been unsuccessful, but that they had sold for the record price of £27,000. Annie Tandey was pleased at the news and said that she wanted to give him something. Annie proceeded to give him the gold-plated casket and decorated scroll, which had been presented to Henry on his being made a Freeman of the Royal Borough of Leamington Spa in 1919, which he duly accepted. Parker took the casket to jewellers to be cleaned, and casually enquired of its value, which he was told was about £9,000. Norman Parker is convinced that, had Annie been aware of the significance and value of this item, it would almost certainly have gone to auction as well. The casket and scroll are now kept in the Mayor's Parlour at Leamington Spa town hall.

In 1981, Frank Cridlan wrote to A.V. Simpson, in the course of which he commented that, following the sale of the medals, the auctioneer had said that he had been in charge of Sotheby's medal section for fourteen years and that it had been the first time he had seen a town attempt to buy the medals of a local VC holder. He added that the auctioneer was 'disappointed we did not succeed'.

Sir Ernest Harrison OBE was the chairman of Racal Electronics, Vodaphone, Chubb Securities and a trustee of the Green Howards' Trust. His original intention had been to leave the medals to the Green Howards in his will, but having visited the Regimental Museum, and seeing its collection of other VC medals, decided to donate them immediately, so that they could be displayed alongside the regiment's other medals; they can now be found in its Medal Room. Sir Ernest Harrison seemed to have completely missed the point that the medals had been awarded when Henry had been a soldier in the Duke of Wellington's Regiment.

The medals were presented to the Green Howards at a ceremony in the Tower of London on Armistice Day in 1997, and accepted on behalf of the regiment by its commanding officer, Lieutenant Colonel Richard Dannatt. Also present at the ceremony was Henry Gordon, Henry's nephew, then 81, who had attended the internment of Henry's ashes at the military cemetery in France. Henry Gordon had not been happy with Annie's decision to sell the medals because he had feared that they would end up in the hands of a private collector. In truth, Henry Gordon would have much preferred the medals to remain within the family, but failing that he was happy for them to go to the Green Howards, saying, 'It is a very happy occasion. All I have wanted is to see this.' But, of course, he was unaware when he said this that Annie had no legal right to sell them in the first place, or indeed that the medals remained the legal property of the Duke of Wellington's Museum.

It also needs to be made clear that the auctioneers, Sir Ernest Harrison and the Green Howards all acted in good faith where the sale of the medals was concerned, and could not have known about the true legal position concerning their ownership.

The presentation of the medals in 1997 sparked yet another round of interest in Henry, who by that time had been dead for twenty years. But once again, the press demonstrated that it felt the story was the alleged incident with Hitler, by the following headlines: 'Hailed by the Führer ... the hero who spared Hitler's life' (*Coventry Evening Telegraph*, 29 July 1997); 'Historians dispute legend that soldier spared Hitler's life' (*Daily Telegraph*, 27 October 1997); 'Don't blame him for saving Hitler' (*Ottawa Citizen*, 29 July 1997); 'A legend under fire: hero couldn't have had Hitler in his sights' (*Daily Mail*, 27 October 1997); 'Hero Henry was just too kind to kill off Hitler' (*The People*, 27 July 1997).

Again, the story and its headlines placed the emphasis on Henry sparing Hitler, rather than his undoubted bravery, and it is perhaps fortunate that Henry was no longer around to experience the renewed media interest.

Despite all that has happened to Henry's medals since 1960 they still remain on the records of the Duke of Wellington's Regiment. As a further twist to this story, the Duke of Wellington's Regiment subsequently noticed that the Green Howards had switched cap badges in a photograph of Henry wearing his medals, so that he was wearing that of the Green Howards. After having this pointed out, however, the photograph was withdrawn.

This was the subject of an exchange of letters between David Tetlow, the curator of the Green Howards Museum, and Major D.L.J. Harrap, Regimental Area Office, Yorkshire Regiment. On 25 July 2006, David Tetlow wrote:

> I have just looked in our medal room and at the moment we have a photograph of Henry Tandey without any medals and a Green Howards cap badge. I've asked the museum assistants to try and locate another photograph where Mr Tandey is wearing the Duke of Wellington's cap badge.

Please note that as a museum professional, ethics dictate that I do not deceive members of the public into thinking that Tandey received these whilst with the Green Howards and I apologise that this has been overlooked in the past.

Some may take the view that in many ways it seems wrong for the medals to reside in the Medal Room of the Green Howards Museum in Richmond, where the public may well come away with the impression that Henry was a member of that regiment at the time he won them, when, of course, that was not the case. The Green Howards Museum's position is that they are pleased and proud to have Henry's medals to display, and perhaps understandably profess no knowledge of what may have gone on before their sale and donation. It seems appropriate, therefore, to at least raise the question: are Henry's medals displayed in the correct museum?

However, life sometimes has a way of sorting things out for the best. If the medals had not been purchased by Sir Ernest Harrison, then the consortium from Leamington Spa would have brought them back for display in the town's museum. Although that would have been better than them being purchased and kept by a private collector, or indeed sold overseas, it is perhaps preferable then that the medals are housed in a museum of one of the two regiments Henry served with. It is important to make the point that at no time have the Duke of Wellington's Regiment sought to question the right of Sir Ernest Harrison to purchase the medals or, indeed, to donate them to the Green Howards.

It is at this point that life intervened, and it did so with a sense of irony: 2006 saw the amalgamation of the Duke of Wellington's and the Green Howards regiments with the Prince of Wales' Own Regiment of Yorkshire to form the new Yorkshire Regiment. The view of the Yorkshire Regiment is that Henry is an important part of their shared history, and that the exact location of his medals is not important, as long as they are held within the regiment as part of its common shared heritage.

Councillor Norman Parker subsequently purchased Henry's dress medals for £1,000 at an auction at Christies, and said:

> They are not the original medals but they are the next best thing. I'm just glad they have returned to Leamington.

★★★

Sadly, nothing is known about what happened to the copy of the Matania painting that hung above Henry and Edith's drawing room fireplace. The clock that was presented to Henry by the Old Contemptibles' Association sits proudly in the lounge of his nephew Henry Gordon's house and is still in perfect working order (plate 27).

★★★

Up until 1984, Leamington Spa had seen five individuals honoured with the award of the VC. The owners of the Regent Hotel, the Cridlan family, named a room within the hotel the VC Lounge, and on 17 November 1980, pictures celebrating the bravery of Henry and Colonel John Cridlan Barrett were unveiled. There was a link between them because Colonel Barrett was the nephew of Mr J.J. Cridlan, a former chairman of the hotel, and Henry had been an employee there before he joined the army. The unveiling of the pictures was performed by Earl Spencer, father of the late Diana, Princess of Wales, and Annie Tandey was also present.

The Cridlan family's connection with the Regent Hotel ended in 1998; the hotel is now a Travelodge, and there is no longer a VC Lounge.

★★★

Following Henry's death, Annie had sold the house in Loudon Avenue and moved to a smaller property. She had spoken of her intention to return to Germany, but that never happened as Annie Tandey died on 15 August 1996 of a heart attack while gardening.

Sadly, there were no children from either of Henry's marriages.

★★★

Very few details are known about the rest of the Tandy family. Magdeline met a soldier, who was home on leave, and subsequently found herself pregnant. Her father was furious and insisted that the couple should marry, which was complicated by the fact that the prospective father, and groom, was Jewish. Inevitably there was a clash of faiths, which resulted in Magdeline moving to London with her son, Henry Gordon.

Henry's brother, Samuel, was in the Merchant Navy and settled in Hartlepool, with his wife and one son. Samuel's son died in the Second World War, and his wife began an affair with another man. These events caused him to begin to drink heavily and eventually his wife had him committed to an asylum, where he remained until he died. Henry's niece, Margaret Riddle, cannot understand why Samuel's many siblings, including Henry, stood back and allowed this to happen to their brother.

Frederick worked in the fishing industry and lived in Hull with his wife Alice, who was disliked by the rest of the family.

George, a homosexual and described as a flamboyant character, moved to London, and seems to have been the one sibling that Henry remained close to.

Edward married a woman by the name of Violet, who, following the marriage, informed him that she had no wish to have any children. Edward was understandably upset, but as Roman Catholic divorce was not an option, leading to an unhappy marriage. Consequently, Violet was another spouse disliked by the family.

Little is known of James, who was known within the family as Bob, other than that towards the end of his life he went to live with Magdeline in London, where he later died.

Florence stayed in Leamington Spa and was briefly married to Thomas O'Connell, but he deserted her soon after the wedding and was never seen or heard of again.

The Tandys, and perhaps this is unsurprising given what has gone before, are remembered as a somewhat dysfunctional family, where serious disagreements were the norm, followed by long periods with little or no contact. Henry was seen as the most sensible and reasonable of them all, but he preferred to keep himself to himself.

Henry was by no means a wealthy man, but he paid for his mother's funeral when she died in 1946. At the time, Catherine was living at 39 Parks Street, Leamington Spa.

★★★

In 2012 Royal Leamington Spa Town Council received planning permission from Warwick District Council to unveil a blue plaque to commemorate Henry Tandey VC DCM MM. This was long overdue, but part of the delay had been pinpointing a suitable location, because over time many of the addresses associated with Henry had disappeared as the town had developed. The plaque was eventually fixed to the wall of the Angel Hotel, Regent Street, which is located near to where Henry's birthplace had stood, on 28 September 2012 when dignitaries and family members came together to celebrate his life, ninety-four years to the day that he won his Victoria Cross.

★★★

Henry had been a courageous soldier, one who served throughout the Great War on the Western Front, was wounded on three occasions and had his bravery rewarded with the three highest decorations he could have received, together with five Mentions in Despatches.

The medal entitlement of Sergeant Henry Tandey, 5th Battalion, Duke of Wellington's Regiment, is given below, taken from the Green Howard's Museum website:

- Victoria Cross (VC)
- Distinguished Conduct Medal (DCM)
- Military Medal (MM)

- 1914 Star – clasp '5th Aug–22nd Nov 1914'
- British War Medal (1914–20)
- Victory Medal (1914–19) – with five palms in recognition of the 5 MIDs
- Defence Medal (1939–45)
- King George VI Coronation Medal (1937)
- Queen Elizabeth II Coronation Medal (1953)
- Queen Elizabeth II Silver Jubilee Medal (1977)

Henry was the most decorated private soldier in the British Army to survive the Great War, and yet anyone paying a visit to either the Imperial War Museum or the National Army Museum will not see anything on display about him. Although both museums hold files on Henry in their archives, and they both have sections of their displays dealing with the Great War, which include material on a number of VC holders, Henry is missing, even though won the VC, DCM and MM within such a short space of time in 1918. The reason for this appears to be that neither museum has any artefacts associated with Henry, but surely a photograph and a display board outlining his military service and achievements is the least that could be expected, given his extraordinary achievements? It echoes the concerns held by his brother, George, in 1963, when he questioned how many people remembered his brother, his bravery and his decorations.

5

The Story of Henry
Tandey and Hitler

In writing a biography of Henry, it is impossible to avoid confronting the story of him allegedly sparing the life of Adolf Hitler. In fact, if 'Henry Tandey' is entered into an Internet search engine it becomes immediately apparent how his name has been firmly linked with that of Hitler through the results that come up, for example: 'How a Right Can Make a Wrong'; 'The Man Who Didn't Shoot Hitler'; 'Henry Tandey: The Man Who Spared Hitler'.

According to the story, at the end of the fighting at Marcoing on 28 September 1918, a wounded and retreating Hitler was seen by a British soldier, Henry, who took aim but chose not to shoot, thus saving the life of the future German Chancellor and architect of the Second World War.

★★★

Apart from the story of Henry sparing Hitler's life, there is within it a further story about how Henry found out about his apparent act of compassion.

The year 1938 was a time of great tension in Europe, and concerns were growing that a second war against the Germans was becoming more and more likely. Henry would almost certainly have been aware that Neville Chamberlain had been to visit Hitler in Munich in September 1938, in an attempt to avert a war, as the prime minister had returned, famously waving a piece of paper and declaring 'peace in our time'.

During his 1938 visit to Hitler, Chamberlain had been invited by him to his Berchtesgaden retreat in Bavaria. It was there that Chamberlain is said to have come across a copy of a painting hanging in Hitler's study, of Allied troops in the First World War, specifically the 2nd Battalion of the Green Howards at Petit Kruiseke on the Ypres–Menin Road, by the Italian artist Fortunino Matania (1881–1963). Intrigued by this, he asked Hitler why such a painting was hanging on his wall, and was told by Hitler, as he pointed to the figure in the front, right foreground:

> That man came so near to killing me that I thought I should never see Germany again, providence saved me from such devilishly accurate fire as those boys were aiming at us.

The figure that Hitler pointed to was Matania's depiction of Private Henry Tandey, and Hitler asked Chamberlain to convey his best wishes and thanks to Henry when he returned to London. On his return from Munich, Chamberlain is said to have telephoned the Tandey household, where the telephone was answered by 9-year-old William Whateley. The Whateleys were related to Edith Tandey, and William was living at the time with the Tandeys at their home in Cope Street due to difficulties within his own immediate family.

William claimed that he called Henry to the telephone, whereupon the prime minister passed on Hitler's message. He recalled that after taking the telephone call 'My uncle recounted it in a matter of fact way', adding that his uncle had always thought there was something familiar about the photographs of Hitler.

There are a number of aspects to this story that, on reflection, are troubling. Firstly, it seems remarkable that, given the situation facing Europe, the British prime minister would have had the time, or perhaps the inclination, to go to the trouble of telephoning Henry.

The second area of concern centres on Henry receiving the telephone call at his home. It would have been unusual in 1938 for private homes, other than those of the affluent, to have a telephone installed. Henry was working for the Triumph Motor Company as a commissionaire and it is possible that the telephone had been installed by his employer. It is possible, but unlikely, that Henry was ex-directory as at that time having your name in the telephone directory was seen as a symbol of status and wealth, and definitely not something to be hidden.

The British Telecommunications (BT) Archive contains a near-complete set of telephone directories for the whole country, produced not only by BT but also by its predecessors, including Post Office Telecommunications, the National Telephone Company and other private companies, which date back to 1880 – the year after the public telephone service was introduced into Great Britain. A search of its records revealed a 1938 directory for Coventry, but Henry's name was not listed. The Triumph Motor Company had three telephone lines in Coventry at this time but none of those were to a domestic address. The addresses listed for the Triumph Motor Company were the Gloria Works, Holbrook Lane (Coventry 8671), the Service Department, Briton Road (Coventry 60251) and the Car Despatch Ordnance Works, Stoney Stanton Road (Coventry 5290).

Henry's niece, Margaret Riddle, has been able to confirm that Henry did indeed live at 22 Cope Street, but that he did not have a domestic telephone. If that is the case then how could the prime minister telephone Henry, and how could William Whateley answer a telephone that did not exist?

Additionally, William's part in this story is interesting because even if Henry had had a domestic telephone at that time, how likely would it have been that a 9-year-old boy who was staying with the Tandeys would have been allowed to answer it? It is more common today to have a telephone answered by a child of a family, but would that have been likely in 1938, when children tended to be seen but not heard?

There are two further points that need to be borne in mind where William's comments are concerned: firstly, he was only 9 at the time of the telephone call, and secondly, there is no way of knowing when his comments were made. The comments do not appear to be those of a young child, and in any event would a boy that age pay enough attention to remember what was said and its importance? It seems more likely, although it cannot be proved, that this was the adult William talking several years later and, presumably, seeking to gain some financial advantage from his association with Henry.

William's recollection of what Henry said, having taken the prime minister's call, is contradicted by Smith (2001), who states that Henry claimed that if he had met Hitler, he certainly did not remember him.

Another area of concern centres on what part, if any, Neville Chamberlain played in this story. The Special Collections, held in the Cadbury Research Centre at the University of Birmingham, hold the Chamberlain Collection. A large part of that collection comprises the papers of Neville Chamberlain, including those concerned with his September 1938 meeting with Hitler.

The university's guide to the Chamberlain Collection states:

> No matter how busy or tired Neville Chamberlain might be, every week he wrote in his own hand a long letter, and every week Ida or Hilda (his sisters) replied to it.

A search through Neville Chamberlain's diaries, journals and letters reveals no reference to Henry at all. In a letter to his sister Ida, written on 19 September 1938, he writes about Hitler's appearance:

> … and altogether he looks entirely undistinguished. You would never notice him in a crowd and would take him for the housepainter he once was.

This comment is interesting for another reason – if Hitler's appearance was such that he was unlikely to be picked out in a crowd, how believable is it that Henry would have recognised him from photographs or newsreels?

Chamberlain's letter also relates that Hitler had paintings by German and Italian artists, and in particular he noted that there was a painting 'of a huge Italian nude' (Charmley, 1989). If Chamberlain noticed the painting of a nude, it seems strange that he would not have noted down in his papers the story that Hitler told of his life being spared by Henry, or, indeed, the presence of a copy of the Matania painting. Even if he was treating it with a pinch of salt, he might have been expected to have recounted the story in a letter to his sisters as an amusing aside; however, the fact that he did not record the story in any way does not prove that it was not something he was told about by Hitler.

The evidence, in my opinion, points to this story of Chamberlain telephoning Henry being almost certainly fictitious. Leaving aside the serious doubts about the truth of how Henry found out, this was an onerous and a difficult period for the prime minister, with many issues beginning to envelope him and place demands on his time and attention, and it stretches belief that he would have found the time or inclination to telephone Henry.

In papers obtained from the Duke of Wellington's Regimental Museum, there is a comment in Henry's regimental biography about rumours beginning to circulate in the press in 1938, that Henry was the man who spared Hitler's life at Marcoing on 28 September 1918. The story did enter the public domain, such as, for example, when on 29 August 1939 Henry received an invitation (*Coventry Evening Telegraph*) from a Blackpool showman, who gave his address as Lore, Glastonbury Avenue, Blackpool, offering him the opportunity 'to exhibit himself as the man who came face to face with Hitler'. Unsurprisingly, Henry declined. The newspaper reported Henry's decision on 12 August 1939, under the heading: 'Coventry VC declines to go on show at Blackpool.'

The means by which Henry had been told that he had spared Hitler's life would have left him just as startled as a telephone call from the prime minister. On 27 April 1941 the *Hindu Madras* newspaper reported on a story that had appeared in the *Montreal Daily Star*. This stated that when Neville Chamberlain had returned to Britain from Munich, he had related what he had been told by Hitler to a colonel in the Green Howards. The circumstances under which this happened are not recorded but it is likely that, whatever the context, the fact of the officer being in the Green Howards triggered some recollection on Chamberlain's part, and he recounted the story, probably in a 'you will never guess what I was told' way. It seems unlikely that Chamberlain attached any credence to the story; nevertheless, the unnamed officer took it upon himself to pass on the news to Henry.

A newspaper article from September 1939, which forms part of a file on Henry held at the Imperial War Museum, reveals that the news had been passed to Henry at a Green Howards regimental reunion held the previous month. The Green Howards Regimental Museum has a collection of back copies of the *Green Howards Gazette*, but unfortunately the one for 1939, which would have included material from that reunion, is the only edition that is missing. It is not possible to know whether Henry was taken aside and given the news, or whether the news was delivered as part of an after-dinner speech. However it was done, it must have come as something of a shock.

Henry seemed to have accepted the news in a reasonably level-headed way, but was also prepared to wait for further information as he said at the time, 'But I shall find out definitely soon I hope.'

★★★

A painting by Matania that at that time hung in the officers' mess of the Green Howards plays an important role in the story of Henry and Hitler.

Hitler is reported to have tasked his staff with searching through British Army records in order to identify the British soldier who saved his life, although just how likely it is that the Germans would have had access to such records is not explained. It seems more likely that Hitler, who retained a keen interest in the Great War and his part in it, had his staff carrying out more general research into his own wartime service. It was during this time that Hitler became aware of the Matania painting hanging in the officers' mess of the Green Howards Regiment.

The likeliest person to have drawn Hitler's attention to the painting was a member of his staff named Dr Schwend. Dr Schwend had served as a medical officer at the First Battle of Ypres in October 1914, and was based in a first aid post close to the Menin Road. What followed is described by Schwend in a letter taken from an *Old Comrades Magazine*, dated 1 March 1937, and reproduced in the *Green Howards Gazette* for April 1937–March 1938, where he recounts that at some point in the fighting he found himself treating a Lieutenant Colonel Earle. The two kept in touch following the war and in December 1936, Earle sent Schwend a colour reproduction of the Matania painting.

Matania, who became a war artist at the outbreak of the First World War working for the British magazine *The Sphere*, was acclaimed for his realistic images of trench warfare. Laffin (1991) described Matania's approach to his paintings:

> He visited the front several times which allowed him to view wartime conditions at first hand and talk with soldiers about their experiences. From sketches and memory he could then finish a painting, often in a few days time. At other times, when his illustrations depicted specific news events he would receive information, photographs or rough sketches and descriptions from on-the-scene reporters or eye-witness reports. Drawing on personal experience and technique as well as on information from archive photographs or prints he would then set to work composing and finishing the required illustration. Rich in detail and carefully composed, his stirring paintings often depicted heroic or romantic scenes.

The Green Howards Regiment commissioned the painting from Matania in 1923. It is based on a sketch of an actual event that took place at the Kruiseke Crossroads, and not the Menin Crossroads, which is about a mile from Gheluvelt (Gilles, 1961). It depicts, in the right foreground, the figure of Henry carrying a wounded soldier on his back.

Unfortunately, the painting is quite often mistakenly thought of as depicting the events at Marcoing that led to Henry's award of the Victoria Cross. This confusion may stem from the painting depicting an event from October 1914, while the key included with the picture names Henry as Private Henry Tandey VC – the award of which stemmed from events in September 1918. The painting now hangs in the Normanby Room at the Green Howards Regimental Museum in Richmond, Yorkshire.

Immediately behind Henry in the painting is a house, and the Green Howards presented the owners, the Van den Broucke family, with a framed print. The print was endorsed:

Presented to the family Van den Broucke by the Green Howards (Alexandra, Princess of Wales Own Yorkshire Regiment) in memory of October 1914.

In the early 1970s the house was demolished when the road was widened and the whereabouts of the print is not known.

In 1937, Hitler, having been alerted to the Matania painting by Schwend, obtained his own copy from Henry's old regiment. The story of how Hitler obtained it was reported in the *Daily Telegraph*, based on an article in the Green Howards Museum's own newsletter. Dr Schwend had written to the Green Howards Regiment requesting a large photo of the painting for Hitler, which was duly sent to him in Germany.

The Green Howards Museum's staff subsequently found a letter from Hitler's adjutant, Captain Weidemann, thanking the regiment for the picture, which was later quoted in the *Daily Telegraph* (28 July 1997):

The Führer is naturally very interested in things connected with his own war experiences. He was obviously moved when I showed him the picture. He has directed me to send you his best thanks for your friendly gift which is so rich in memories.

According to the story, Hitler identified Henry from the painting. It is not known whether Hitler received any explanation about the figures in the painting, but somehow he came to know that the figure in the right foreground was Henry. Anyone who has stood in front of the painting (plate 6) and studied the depiction of Henry, and then looked at his photograph (plate 9), together with those written descriptions of his physical attributes, will realise that there is no similarity. The likelihood is that Hitler was drawn to the painting because it depicted his own first experience of fighting on the Western Front, and only subsequently did he discover the link to Henry.

Another version of the story is that Hitler had identified Henry from newspaper photographs printed around the time that he received the VC. These photographs, similar to the one on the cover of this book, would have been grainy, in black and white, and not at all to the quality of today's digital photography, so it somewhat stretches credibility that Hitler should have identified him from those, or indeed linked these images to the one in the painting.

***

Henry had been accompanied to the Green Howards reunion in August 1939 by Edith, who had never seen the original painting before, although she had a print of it hanging above her drawing room fireplace. According to the *Coventry Herald* on 5 August 1939, on showing Edith the painting, Henry said, 'This is where I defied Hitler' – maybe the word 'apparently' somehow got lost in the reporting. The interesting word here is 'defied', which conveys resistance to the German advance, of which he believed Hitler was a part, rather than a sense of resisting a specific enemy soldier, or indeed sparing his life.

A print of the painting now hangs in the Union Jack Club, near Waterloo station in London, which houses a number of pictures to do with VC holders. The framed print had belonged to Henry Gordon who was persuaded to let it go to the Union Jack Club, which then paid for it to be cleaned.

★★★

From what he subsequently said, Henry seemed certain, at least initially, that if the event had happened at all then it had occurred in or around the Menin Crossroads in October 1914, and not at Marcoing in September 1918. In the 1939 article he takes up the story:

> We were dug in by the Menin Cross Roads with orders to stay there whatever happened. The Germans were holding the ridge nine hundred yards in front, with sixteen machine guns to our two – and behind one of the guns was the future leader of the German nation. I didn't know he was there of course. No-one but his own company knew that Corporal [sic] Hitler existed.

He then added about Hitler: 'But if he says he was then I suppose he must have been.' This could be interpreted as naivety on Henry's part but more probably reflects the fact that, as his family recall, he did not take the story seriously, and so was speaking with his tongue firmly in his cheek.

Henry went on to describe some of the ensuing action:

> Did I see Hitler? I had the sights of my rifle on most of their gun crews, but whether I hit any of them I shall never know. I've wondered since how near I came to knocking down the future dictator.

The above description by Henry is of him and his comrades under attack and pinned down, where he is actively seeking to shoot the Germans manning the machine guns, rather than choosing not to shoot at those retreating beaten, wounded and unarmed. Hitler himself seems to agree with this, as he referred in his comments to Chamberlain about the 'devilishly accurate fire as those boys were aiming at us'.

The two key players in this story were, for a very brief spell, in action at around the same time near Gheluvelt but, according to Weber, Hitler was at that time a simple infantryman. There is no mention in the works of Weber, Williams or Kershaw that Hitler ever fired a machine gun or was part of a machine-gun crew, and he himself never claimed to have been part of one either.

It is quite possible that separate events, occurring four years apart, have either accidentally or deliberately been fused together to produce the story of Henry's act of compassion. Henry, though, sounded less than convinced by what he had been told when, in an article in the *Coventry Herald* on 5 August 1939, he commented:

> According to them, I've met Adolf Hitler. Maybe they're right but I can't remember him. So I've met the dictator and taken no notice of him.

The above comment directly contradicts William Whateley's claim of what Henry had said after having been 'telephoned' by Neville Chamberlain.

★★★

As Henry discovered more about the story of his apparent act of compassion, he seemed to accept the possibility that it could have happened, but was never to be totally convinced of its absolute truth, and eventually he stopped taking it seriously at all. Nevertheless, the possibility that he might have spared Hitler's life did cause him to doubt his disbelief of the story, and this at times left him feeling some sense of responsibility. On these occasions, as events in Europe unfolded, he found himself living with the awful thought that if the story was true, then, by pulling the trigger, he could have changed the course of history and saved millions of lives. It is open to others to debate whether Hitler's death in 1918 would have in fact prevented the Second World War.

Henry initially thought that the story related to October 1914 and the German machine-gun crews, but by 1940 he seemed to be entertaining the idea of a different scenario; this might have been because he had received the further information he was hoping to hear about back in August 1939. This change of setting, which involved him sparing the life of a wounded, unarmed and retreating Hitler, seemed plausible to Henry because, as he later told journalists, he had never shot wounded soldiers, and there is some evidence that this practice did occur on the Western Front.

Having been told that he had spared the life of Hitler, Henry was prepared to entertain the possibility of the story being true when he told a journalist from the *Sunday Graphic*, shortly after the bombing of Coventry:

> I didn't like to shoot at a wounded man but if I'd known who this corporal [sic] would turn out to be if he'd got off, I'd give ten years now to have five minutes clairvoyance then.

It must be remembered, though, that this was a low point for the country and for Coventry, and Henry can be excused for feeling a little sorry for himself and emotional after the sights he had witnessed, including having his own home destroyed. It might equally be true that the journalist concerned took Henry's comments out of context, which might go some way to explaining his distrust of the press.

Brown (2001) includes a number of quotations from British soldiers, which show that sparing a wounded and defeated enemy was not an unusual occurrence, as can be seen from the following:

> I had sworn to shoot the first (Hun) I saw, but could not bring myself to it. I am a sentimental ass. (Lieutenant A. Wilkinson, 2nd Battalion, Coldstream Guards)

Or from Lieutenant A.G. May, who failed to shoot a German when 'he saw the somewhat inadequate specimen of the hated enemy who had appeared in his sights'. The Reverend Montague Blere is quoted as having 'come across instances of soldiers who held fire when they had the enemy at their mercy'.

There is, then, some evidence, based on the practice of others, to support Henry's comment that he had never shot a wounded German soldier, and so it must have seemed at least feasible to him that amongst those he had spared, one of them could have been Hitler.

An article in the *Ottawa Citizen* on 29 July 1997, under a heading of 'Don't blame him for saving Hitler', quoted a friend of Henry's, Major Robert Metcalfe, who said:

> If he had not been such a decent man, he would have just shot and killed another German Soldier.

He also went on to give the following view of Henry saying:

> He was a very quiet chap. Not too big, but friendly, and certainly brave.

★★★

It is also important to bear in mind that there are a number of combinations of what possibly did occur. Firstly, Hitler may have had his life spared by a British soldier who was Henry Tandey. Secondly, Hitler had his life spared by a British soldier who was not Henry Tandey. Thirdly, Hitler simply made the story up for his own purposes. There is no evidence or discernible motivation for Henry to have made a claim that he had saved Hitler's life – what possible advantage could accrue as a result to this quiet and proud man?

But did it happen? There are two approaches that could be applied to test out the validity of the story; namely, can the story be verified beyond reasonable doubt or, on the balance of probabilities, is it likely to be true?

Without documentary evidence or first-hand testimony there is no way of establishing whether this happened beyond reasonable doubt, as the two individuals concerned are now dead and there are no eyewitness accounts in support of it. It can be verified beyond doubt that Henry was at Marcoing on 28 September 1918, as he was awarded the VC for his actions that day.

In 1997, it was reported that the Regimental Secretary of the Green Howards Regiment, Lieutenant Colonel Neil McIntosh, had investigated this story and as a result had contacted the Bavarian State Archives in Munich. McIntosh received confirmation from the Bavarian State Archives on 20 October 1997 (since confirmed, following a request for information for this book), in a letter held at the Regimental Museum, that Hitler was on leave from the 25–27 September 1918, returning to the front on the 28th, meaning he was either on his way back at the time of the incident or was some miles away, making it unlikely that the incident could have occurred. This left him to say:

> I'm afraid this delightful little story is untrue.

In a letter from David Harrop, of the Green Howards, to Mr G. Mahoney of the USA, dated 11 August 2006, there is further clarification of the information received from Germany. According to this letter, Hitler's regiment was transferred on 17 September 1918 from the Favreuil–Bapaume sector to Wytschaete, about 50 miles north of Marcoing. This means that Hitler was either on leave or returning from leave at the time, or with his regiment 50 miles north of Marcoing; therefore, he and Henry could not have crossed paths on 28 September.

McIntosh is quoted in the *Yorkshire Post* (29 July 1997) as going on to dispute whether Henry received a telephone call from Chamberlain, but for reasons other than the fact that there was no telephone at 22 Cope Street:

> This legend is based on an article that appeared soon after Tandey's house in Coventry had been bombed and he came out with this story. Old soldiers are the same the world over, they tend to embellish. Tandey may have invented this story and on the other hand he may not.
>
> But we have no evidence to support it and there's no reason why we should because at the time he was serving with the Duke of Wellington's Regiment.

These comments are interesting because McIntosh seems to cast doubt on Henry's integrity. Rather than supporting Henry, he readily passes any responsibility for verifying the story over to the Duke of Wellington's, at a time when the Green Howards Regimental Museum must have known it was going to receive his medals. There is no evidence that Henry was at all boastful, or was someone who embellished the truth. And again it is worth asking the question as to what possible advantage there would have been in inventing such a story.

McIntosh wrote a number of letters to newspapers, and to individuals, where he further elaborated on this story. On 20 November 2000 he wrote to Robert Matthew of the *Sunday Telegraph*, quite happily saying that 'it was me who "rubbished" the story', and went on to say:

Tandey made his outrageous statement when he was in an emotional state, his house in Coventry having been bombed by the Luftwaffe. It should be noted that he had not made such a statement in the previous twenty-two years.

McIntosh wrote to Major Robert Metcalfe about the same time, saying that the story was 'a load of rubbish unfortunately'. The thrust of McIntosh's argument is that the whole story originated with Henry himself in 1940, but, as has been established earlier in this chapter, this was clearly not the case.

There is evidence, taken from newspaper cuttings held at the Imperial War Museum, that Henry talked publicly for the first time about the incident in 1939, over a year earlier than McIntosh had suggested, when, although he was, in all likelihood, shocked and bemused by what he had just learnt, he did not seem to be in what could be described as an emotional state. If he did not know about the incident until 1939, how could he have spoken about it over the previous twenty-two years?

All in all, McIntosh appears, therefore, to have been mistaken in some of his assertions. Interestingly, there was some disagreement about these matters within the Green Howards Museum fraternity itself because Major Roger Chapman, spokesperson for the regiment, said of Henry (*Daily Telegraph*, 28 July 1997):

> He was a remarkably brave man, small, only 5 foot 5 inches and 119 pounds, and intensely modest. He was no line shooter. After a lot of research, we have no doubts he did meet up with Hitler and allowed him to live, an act of compassion he regretted 22 years later.

The key phrase in the above quote is 'After a lot of research', but it is difficult to see the basis for such a strong statement. It is interesting to note that in his 2001 publication, which tells the story of each of the regiment's VC holders (although, strictly speaking, Henry was not one of them), Chapman makes no mention of Henry's alleged meeting with Hitler which appears odd because surely, if the research had been carried out, it is not unreasonable to think that this aspect of Henry's story would have been mentioned, due to its 'sensational' nature.

McIntosh was correct in advocating that the facts of the matter could not be proved beyond reasonable doubt, but in doing so he was wrong to impugn Henry's character and integrity, as Henry had been unaware of the story until 1939.

★★★

The story, therefore, cannot be proved beyond reasonable doubt, so, using the balance of probabilities test, how likely is it to have occurred? If it had occurred, the event probably happened on a battlefield where the weather and drifting smoke would not have helped visibility. If it happened on 28 September, when Henry won his VC, then it had to have been later in the day because his citation refers to 'later in the evening', when fighting was still taking place with darkness drawing on.

The citation also states that Henry was wounded twice, receiving wounds to both an arm and a leg, and was faint from loss of blood. So, the chances are that at that stage in the day, when the fighting was over, it would have been a time when Henry's main concern would have been getting his wounds tended to. The nature of his wounds, described as 'nasty' by Private Lister, were serious enough for him to be hospitalised, and he was not deemed fit for service again until March 1919.

Hitler's claims about being spared by any Allied soldier cannot be verified, let alone confirmed that it was Henry. There is no information as to how far away the soldier concerned was from Hitler, and it is quite likely that both men would have been dirty and dishevelled.

Hitler claimed to have recognised Henry from a newspaper report on his award of the VC, which contained his photograph, but this was not published until fifteen months after their paths are said to have crossed, as Henry received his award in December 1919. How likely is it that Hitler could have recognised Henry, as has already been said, from a black-and-white newspaper photograph, which would not have been to the standards of today's digital technology?

In an article in the *Daily Telegraph*, dated 23 December 1977, which appeared on the day of his funeral, Henry is quoted as having said, although there is no indication of when or where he did so:

> Because Hitler was wounded he was not closely watched and escaped back to his own lines.

Interestingly, thirty-seven years before, in the *Sunday Graphic* of 1 December 1940, Henry gave a slightly different version:

> For several days I and my platoon had held up a large German contingent with our two Lewis guns. The Germans had sixteen machine guns but one by one we picked off the members of the gun crews. Eventually we decided to finish these Jerries off, so I rigged up a plank bridge for the others to get across and charge them. This 'rigging up the plank bridge' meant fifteen minutes cool work under a hail of machine gun fire from the enemy. Then we dashed across. Only nine of us made it. We were hopelessly outnumbered so I told the boys to fix bayonets and charge. The Germans fled and we took 37 prisoners.

> The departing Jerries were led by a corporal, I was going to pick him
> off but he was wounded and I didn't like to shoot a wounded man.

This quotation, again if accurate, paints a somewhat different picture
of the event to the one put forward by Hitler, because in his version
there is no mention of capture. Although it can be assumed that
Hitler would not have wanted to further the idea that he had been
captured, and as tempting as it might be to relish the picture of
him having surrendered and been taken prisoner, the fact is that he
was not in the front line because he was a regimental headquarters
despatch runner. Also, Hitler was gassed and not wounded in the
conventional sense, which implies some form of external injury.

Also needing to be borne in mind is the description of Hitler
from his First World War service (Williams):

> Photographs of him during the war show a thin, gaunt face dominated
> by a thick, dark, bushy moustache. He was usually on the edge of his
> group, expressionless where others were smiling.

How recognisable would the Hitler of the 1930s have been as that
man? And how recognisable would he have been to Henry, who
supposedly saw him just once at the end of a long day of fighting? It is
useful to include in this argument Neville Chamberlain's description
of Hitler in 1938, which was quoted earlier, as a further counter to
stories of Henry himself thinking Hitler looked familiar.

There are no records of Henry having spoken publicly about the
incident involving Hitler after 1940, and, especially in the aftermath
of the Second World War, this would not have been something to
talk about. There is no evidence that those around Henry, or indeed
Henry himself, took the story seriously. By keeping quiet, Henry
must have hoped that the whole business would simply blow over. His
policy of not talking about it seems to have worked because the story
only came to the fore again at his death in 1977, and again in 1997
when his medals were presented to the Green Howards Regimental
Museum. The story panders to the media's need for sensationalism,

and it is certain that Henry would have been dismayed to see what he probably regarded as a joke being regurgitated as if it was fact.

★★★

Hitler viewed himself as the saviour of Germany, and among his many other traits were those of self-delusion and self-mythology. He had the ability to convince himself of his version of the truth and then, in turn, to convince others, quite often by the re-writing of history. This was evident from an early age and continued, as Weber argues, into later life, an example being the origins of the German national anthem. According to Weber, in *Mein Kampf* Hitler claimed to have heard the soldiers around him in October 1914 chanting '*Deutschland, Deutschland uber alles*', the words of the German national anthem. Weber disputes this and points to some detailed letters that Hitler wrote, in the period December 1914 to February 1915, where he discussed the fighting but made no mention of the men chanting at all.

Hitler consistently painted a portrait of himself as a front-line soldier in the thick of the action, and in this he was aided by many of his contemporaries writing in the late 1920s and early 1930s. But Weber, in his revisionist study of Hitler in the Great War, writes persuasively that the truth was consistently different, as revealed in contemporary documents written in the period 1914–18. The contrast between what was written in these two periods appears stark. In 1914–18, Hitler was unknown, other than to those he served with, and was unlikely to have made an impression on those around him of being a man destined for future greatness, and therefore worth noting. The later writing came from a period when Hitler was on the way to power, and those penning the alternative history of his wartime experience wanted to curry favour, as well as having their own agendas.

Whether he had been spared by an Allied soldier or not, the story would have been invaluable in building up the myth that he had been saved for a greater purpose, namely restoring Germany to what Hitler saw as its true position in the world. Indeed, an article in the *Northern Echo* on 25 October 1997, under a heading of 'Hitler was in my sights story by VC soldier is debunked', states that the Green Howards Museum believed that the story probably originally surfaced as a piece of wartime propaganda. If Hitler was telling such a story, then how much better would it have sounded if it was embellished by the claim that the man concerned was the most decorated private soldier to survive the First World War, rather than some anonymous, yet still heroic, Tommy whose bravery had not attracted the same attention? It is likely, therefore, that it was a calculated decision on Hitler's part to implicate Henry, given his profile as a flesh-and-blood hero who had survived the Western Front.

It is also interesting that Williams, in writing about Hitler's First World War service, never mentioned this incident anywhere in his book, which is comprehensive in all other respects. There is barely a mention of Henry in any of the major biographies on Hitler. Weber refers to it in his book, briefly, as an unlikely story.

★★★

This story continues to attract interest from a variety of individuals. In 2007–08, John Bird wrote a play entitled *Trusting Herr Schickelgruber*, which centres on Hitler's meeting with Neville Chamberlain in 1938. In the course of the play, Hitler explains the story of his meeting with Henry, and the playwright uses the device of Chamberlain's fictional secretary, who had not only served in the Great War but actually fought alongside Henry, to talk about his character. To date, this play still awaits its first performance.

★★★

Amongst the papers relating to Henry held at the Green Howards Museum is the transcript of the article from the *Sunday Graphic* of 1 December 1940. The article is, to some extent, confusing. In the first paragraph, it starts by saying that the incident happened on 28 September 1918, but then goes on to describe events as taking place at Menin in October 1914. This article seems to epitomise the confusion, poor reporting and research that surrounds this story, and how, over the years, mistakes and wrong assumptions, if repeated often enough, can become facts.

The article is based on an interview given to the newspaper by Henry and is riddled with a number of minor errors such as spelling mistakes, but it is, nevertheless, interesting. Henry is clearly talking about the events at Marcoing, as his version of events corresponds to the description in his citation for the VC. So, where did the reference to Menin come from? Menin and Marcoing are separated by a number of miles and, in terms of the two actions involved, by four years.

There remains a remote, if unlikely, possibility that the alleged incident may have occurred in October 1914 at the First Battle of Ypres, which was both Henry and Hitler's introduction to action in the Great War. This was certainly Henry's initial view and this may, in turn, have been based on the information passed to him by Neville Chamberlain via the officer at the August 1939 reunion.

The story of Henry sparing Hitler's life at Marcoing on 28 Septemeber 1918 is just that, a story. Having applied the two tests, based on what is known or can be surmised, it can be confidently stated that the alleged incident between Hitler and Henry cannot be proved, either beyond reasonable doubt or on the balance of probabilities, to have occurred on 28 September 1918.

Epilogue

Research inevitability produces more questions than answers, and that is certainly the case where the life of Henry Tandey is concerned. I have had to rely largely on secondary sources in order to build up a picture of his war, based on the experiences of others on the Western Front, because Henry either did not keep a diary or write letters from the front, or they have simply not survived. I am extremely grateful to the very many authors for their work, which I have been able to draw on in order to explore the world of the Western Front – the centre of Henry's life for four long years.

It is my belief that when researching there is a need to have, what I term, a 'proper curiosity' about the information that you come across and you must be prepared to follow it, although, frustratingly, it may lead to a dead end. An example of where this approach resulted in something positive was the discovery of a small newspaper clipping about Henry's funeral, which gave the name of the firm of undertakers involved. In a telephone call to Pargetter and Son I found myself talking to Mr Pargetter, who was prepared to spend time retrieving Henry's file, and then spoke to me about the funeral and his firm's involvement in the burial of his ashes in France. He also put me in touch with Henry's family doctor, John Maclean, who had regularly visited Henry throughout the last stages of his life. Although Dr Maclean was unable to remember much about his patient, he did have a Christmas card that had been sent by Henry and Annie in 1976 – poignantly Henry's last Christmas – which he very kindly passed on to me. The Gordon family confirmed that the card had been signed by Henry, and I have subsequently passed it on to the family.

On another occasion, I came across a newspaper clipping about a memorial service for VC holders that was being organised by Peter Elkin at Lichfield Cathedral in 2007. I was able to contact Peter Elkin and he kindly forwarded a letter from me to those relatives of Henry who had contacted him. As I result I was contacted by Tony Gordon, who is a great nephew of Henry on the Tandey side of the family.

Tony Gordon has been immensely helpful and I cannot thank him enough, as through his talking to his father, Henry's nephew Henry Gordon, and other relatives, he has been able to provide some interesting and valuable information, together with photographs. I have been able to add this material to the book, and, on occasion, the information he has been able to supply has stopped me from making factual errors. Through Tony I was able to meet his father and hear, first hand, his memories of Henry Tandey. Henry Gordon bears a striking physical similarity to his uncle, and I believe they share similar personalities, so it was a remarkable experience to meet him.

Contact with members of the Gordon family was a valuable development in my research because, up to that point, I had only been able to speak to a great nephew and two great nieces on the Whateley side of the family. The Whateleys were related to Henry through marriage and consequently, although enthusiastic in their support of my book, were limited in what they were able to tell me.

I am certain that scattered around the country there are individuals, either family members or friends, who will have documents, photographs, recollections or indeed artefacts relating to Henry, but who may not realise their significance in helping to provide as complete a picture as possible of him. I hope that by writing this book it will encourage those people to come forward and share what they know, before the inevitable passage of time makes it too late. In doing so they may be able to help fill in the gaps in Henry's story, or, indeed, correct any mistakes or misrepresentations that I may have made.

So, as a result of writing this book, what do I believe I know about Henry, and where are the gaps?

In terms of his early years, the facts are that Henry was the eldest child of parents who lived in Leamington Spa, he attended St Peter's School for Boys, he went to work at the Regent Hotel in 1909 and he joined the army in 1910, which represents a short list spanning the first nineteen years of his life. There are, inevitably, a number of aspects of his life from that period that are unclear, which are outlined below.

Henry disclosed that he had spent time in an orphanage in details that he supplied to the Victoria Cross Association. There were many times when I wished that he had kept this information to himself, as I spent much time and effort trying, fruitlessly as it turned out, to identify the establishment concerned, the regime involved, the reasons why he found himself in such a place and the effect it had on him. To date, I have not been able to establish anything about this episode of his life and it has, therefore, taken on the guise of what can be best described as an inconvenient truth.

There is also much that is unknown about the Tandy family, and in particular Henry's relationship with his father, which may or may not have contributed to him spending time in an orphanage or workhouse. The Tandys were not a family that ever sat down and talked, and so the bulk of their family history has simply disappeared as Henry's siblings have died.

For Henry, his years in the army have proved more straightforward to research, as his service record exists together with his medal citations. As a result of that I was able to track, with what I hope is reasonable accuracy, where he was throughout 1914–18. I had no wish to write another book on the Western Front, but it did seem appropriate to discuss the uniform, conditions and life of the soldiers throughout the conflict on the Western Front in a general way because, although Henry appears not to have written about these things himself, he was there and must have shared those experiences.

I do not know with any certainty why he chose to join the army in 1910 but I sense, although I might be wrong, that part of his decision may have been based on his feeling that the army would provide an alternative family, given the strong hints of troubles in that part of his life, as well the promise of adventure, travel and a degree of financial security.

Henry was proud of his association with the army, which he described, at the time of re-enlisting in 1919, as 'the finest thing in the world for a young man', but it appears that there were times when he was not entirely happy in the Green Howards, and is quoted as saying that he felt he was being denied opportunities for recognition with that regiment, although, sadly, he never went into detail about this. In later life, Henry revealed that he experienced jealousy from his comrades in the Duke of Wellington's caused almost certainly by the way he was excused parades, fatigues and drills following the award of his gallantry medals. At first glance it seems strange, therefore, that he should have re-enlisted in a regiment where he was experiencing problems, but it is likely these would not have started until after his re-enlistment, when, perhaps the other soldiers saw his special treatment as unfair because they did not fully appreciate the nature of the man and what he had achieved. It is also true that in any organisation, including the armed forces, individuals will have experienced jealousy and a lack of recognition, so it merely shows that Henry was just subject to the feelings that everyone might get from time to time – he was human just like the rest of us.

There is also the reference in his discharge papers to Henry having a drinking problem, but there is, again, no explanation as to what had led to that comment being made. Henry's family are adamant that he was not a heavy drinker and saw such comments as a straightforward case of snobbery, with the officers concerned feeling the need to say something negative to, in effect, put him in his place. There is no definitive evidence either way, but my sense is of a man who did not ordinarily drink more than the odd half pint, and enjoyed the regimental reunions where he could relax with other veterans in a situation where drink tended to flow, and on those occasions he could end up 'tiddly'. Ending up 'tiddly' at regimental reunions is not in itself evidence of a problem with alcohol.

The picture of Henry that emerges is of someone who had a strong work ethic, led a quiet life, but enjoyed reunions and the events associated with being a VC holder. I also believe he saw attendance as a duty to those who were killed in the Great War and would never be able to attend themselves.

The period from 1926 to the end of Henry's life, because it is relatively recent, has produced more certainty. Henry spent the rest of his working life as a commissionaire with (Standard) Triumph Motors, and lived in Coventry. After the death of his first wife, Edith, he married Annie Whateley, but sadly there were no children from either marriage. Family and acquaintances remember him as a quiet man with a sense of humour, who was happy to be on the periphery rather than at the centre of family events. He is also remembered as someone prepared to help family and acquaintances out when the need arose. In later life, he was not a particularly happy man but I feel that, understandably, such unhappiness stemmed from a combination of his second marriage, the onset of severe arthritis and his final battle with terminal cancer.

A number of questions still remain, particularly the nature of the relationship between Henry and Annie. I believe it was a marriage of convenience, with not too much affection on either of their parts; an assertion that appears to be borne out of the recollections of the family, Henry's surgeon and her failure to attend the burial of his ashes at Masnières.

This, in turn, leads me to the sale of his medals. I feel that I 'know' the story of the sale of Henry's medals, based upon my interpretation of the information available. There seems to be, perhaps, an academic debate to be had regarding the ownership of the medals, which now appear to be on display in the 'wrong' regimental museum, but the position of the Yorkshire Regiment is clear on this point. The regiment, which now includes the Green

Howards and the Duke of Wellington's, is not concerned about where the medals are located as long as they are held within the regiment somewhere.

It remains a mystery as to why Henry did not return his medals to the Duke of Wellington's in 1960, and, therefore, it stands as an aspect of his life where his actions can be questioned. I am sure that Henry would not have wanted his medals to have been sold. However, if they were not to remain in the family then it is preferable, and Henry would have wanted this, that they are displayed in a regimental museum, rather than be in the hands of a private collector.

I am certain, based on my research, that Henry and Hitler did not cross paths in September 1918 at Marcoing. There remains a remote, if unlikely, chance that the incident could have occurred in October 1914. If it had happened then the chances of either Henry or Hitler being able to identify one another after many years had passed seem remarkably low. Hitler may well have had his life spared when wounded, unarmed and retreating from the battlefield, but it seems incredibly unlikely that it was Henry who had spared his life.

Henry's recollections tend to show that he was initially prepared to entertain the possibility that it had occurred, based upon what he had been told in August 1939, but from then onwards he seemed to be talking about events of October 1914. This was due to his mistaken belief that Hitler formed part of a machine-gun crew at that time. I think that as the years passed, Henry saw the whole thing as a joke, which he rarely, if ever, spoke about.

Based upon what I have read about Hitler, it seems to me that he had engaged in spinning a web of self-mythology which, in turn, at the hands of the Nazi propaganda machine, was accepted by the German people and thus became a national myth. As part of that myth, Hitler claimed that his life had been providentially spared so that he could later go on to save the German nation. Two salient points emerged from my brief overview of Hitler's life. Firstly, that he was prepared to resort to pretence to achieve his ends, and secondly, that he was, in later life, prepared to state a different version of reality when it suited him. He lived in what

Kershaw describes as an 'egoistic fantasy world'. It is a reasonable conclusion to reach, therefore, that Hitler could well have lied about this, given that in 1918 he was said to be 'a psychopath with symptoms of hysteria'.

Propaganda was an important tool of Hitler and the Third Reich, so it is possible that he chose to embellish many aspects of his Great War service, including the story of his life being spared, which may have been true, by claiming that his life had been saved by the most decorated British private soldier to have survived the Great War. It would have played to Hitler's ego to enhance the story in this way, rather than stop at saying that his life had been spared by an anonymous soldier, who may or may not even have been British.

I am confident that I have unravelled how Henry first heard the news that he had spared Hitler's life. The accepted version is that the prime minister, Neville Chamberlain, telephoned him, and yet there are no records that show the Tandey household had a telephone.

A search of the Chamberlain Collection did not reveal anything to support the story that Neville Chamberlain was told the story by Hitler in September 1938, or that he, in turn, then contacted Henry. And yet, newspaper articles from 1939 show that Neville Chamberlain had been told this story by Hitler, and that following his return from Munich he told the story to an officer of the Green Howards. The circumstances under which Chamberlain recounted the story to the officer, and how this was passed on to Henry, are unknown, other than that it happened at a Green Howards reunion in August 1939. It does seem to be the case that a story repeated often enough assumes the mantle of facts; an issue where media coverage of this aspect of Henry's life has been concerned.

The one thing over which there can be no doubt, as the various medal citations show, is that Henry was an extremely brave man, a 'hero of the old berserk type', and men and women like him are still needed today if battles and wars are to be won.

In a sense, I have lived with Henry Tandey for a couple of years now, and he has never been far from my mind as this project has developed. I am pleased to say that I have grown to like and respect this man based on my research, but I am not blind to the possibility that like any of us he almost certainly had his flaws.

I would like more people to have a chance of learning about his bravery and the award of the VC, DCM and MM he received for exploits that occurred in a few short weeks between the end of August and the end of September 1918. Neither the Imperial War Museum nor the National Army Museum has anything about Henry on display within their Great War exhibits. It would seem fitting, therefore, that both museums should include some information on Henry so that their visitors are able to see and learn something about this unique man.

Now that the book is finished, there are a number of things that I hope to have achieved. Firstly, I hope that I have done justice to the life of this ordinary man who displayed extraordinary bravery. Secondly, I hope, perhaps optimistically, that Henry will, as a result, now be known for his bravery and not for the alleged incident with Hitler. Thirdly, I hope that I have produced an interesting read, whether for First World War historians or those simply wanting to know more about this man. And lastly, I hope that others may be encouraged to help fill the remaining gaps in Henry's story.

Appendix I

Henry Tandey's Military Service Record

Taken from a letter dated 27 January 1978 from the Ministry of Defence to the Regimental Secretary of the Duke of Wellington's Regiment, part of the Lummis File held in the Templer Study Centre of the National Army Museum. The Reverend Canon William M. Lummis MC, Rural Dean of Hingham, Norfolk, a former captain in the Suffolk Regiment, compiled files on VC holders for the Military Historical Society.

Regiment	Action	Date
	Enlisted in the Yorkshire Regiment of the regular army	12.08.1910
	Joined at Richmond	15.08.1910
Green Howards	Served with the 2nd Battalion	23.01.1911– 24.10.1916
	Served with the 3rd Battalion	05.05.1917– 10.06.1917

	Served with the 9th Battalion	11.06.1917– 27.11.1917
	Served with the 3rd Battalion	23.01.1918– 14.03.1918
	Served with the 12th Battalion	15.03.1918– 25.07.1918
	Transferred to Duke of Wellington's Regiment	26.07.1918
Duke of Wellington's	Served with the 5th Battalion	27.07.1918 – 04.10.1918
	Discharged	14.03.1919
	Re-enlisted in 3rd Battalion the Duke of Wellington's Regiment	15.03.1919
	Appointed Unpaid Acting L/Cpl	18.03.1919
	Posted to the 2nd Battalion	04.02.1921
	Reverted to private at own request	08.02.1921
	Discharged – services no longer required	05.01.1926

OVERSEAS SERVICE

France	05.10.1914–24.10.1916 11.06.1917–21.09.1917 15.03.1918–04.10.1918
Gibraltar	11.04.1922–18.02.1923
British Forces in Turkey	19.02.1923–23.08.1923
Egypt	24.08.1923–29.09.1925

Appendix II

Significant Events Attended by Henry Tandey Post-1918

17.12.1918	VC presented by George V at Buckingham Palace
08.06.1946	Victory Parade in Whitehall Dinner at the Dorchester Hotel
24.07.1958	First reunion dinner of the VC/GC Association at the Café Royal
07.07.1960	Second reunion dinner of the VC/GC Association at the Café Royal
17.07.1962	A reception for the VC/GC Association at Buckingham Palace, in the presence of Queen Elizabeth II Banquet given by the Rt Hon. the Lord Mayor of London to the VC/GC Association at the Mansion House
18.07.1962	Third Reunion Dinner at the Café Royal
15.07.1964	First memorial service at St Martins in the Field A reception for the VC/GC Association by the prime minister, Sir Alec Douglas-Home, at 10 Downing Street

16.07.1964	Fourth reunion dinner
13.07.1966	Second memorial service at St Martins in the Field
14.07.1966	Fifth reunion dinner
18.07.1968	Third memorial service at St Martins in the Field
19.07.1968	Sixth reunion dinner
01.07.1976	Parade in Leamington Spa on the sixtieth anniversary of the first day of the Battle of the Somme

In addition, Henry attended the funeral of W. Amey VC on 1 June 1940 at All Saints church, Leamington Spa, and the funeral of A. Hutt VC on 20 April 1954 at Canley Crematorium, Coventry

Bibliography

This is a list of the works quoted or used for specific reference purposes:
The Lummis Collection, held at the National Army Museum, London
File on Henry Tandey VC, held at the Imperial War Museum, London
File on Henry Tandey VC held at the Green Howards Regimental
Museum, Richmond, North Yorkshire
Papers on Henry Tandey VC, supplied by the Duke of Wellington's
Regimental Museum, Halifax
Documents supplied by the Victoria Cross Society
Quotation from *After the Victorians* by A.N. Wilson, published by
Hutchinson, reproduced by permission of The Random House
Group Ltd.
OUP material: *Hitler's First War* by T. Weber (2010), sixty-four
words from pp. 53, 204, 212, 215 and 221 by permission of Oxford
University Press.
Extracts from *A Storm in Flanders* by W. Groom reproduced by
permission of Cassell, a division of the Orion Publishing Group,
London. © Winston Groom, 2002
Extracts from *Blindfold and Alone* by C. Corns and J. Hughes-Wilson
reproduced by permission of Cassell, a divsion of the Orion Publishing
Group, London. © Catherine Corns and John Hughes-Wilson, 2001

1 AN ACT OF COMPASSION REPAID?

Coventry Evening Telegraph

Gardiner, J. (2011), *The Blitz: The British Under Attack*, Harper Press, London

Gilbert, M. (2008), 'The Bombing of Coventry: the real story', *The Times*

McGory, M. (2008), *The Coventry Blitz, Coventry and Warwickshire News*, CWN/Heritage/The Coventry Blitz

The Sunday Graphic, 1 December 1940

Wilson, A.N. (2005), *After the Victorians: 1901–1953*, Hutchinson, London

2 THE EARLY YEARS.

Bullock, A. (1973), *Hitler: A Study in Tyranny*, Hamlyn Publishing Group

Carver, M. (2000), *The Boer War*, Pan Books, London

Crompton, F. (1997), *Workhouse Children*, Sutton Publishing Ltd, Stroud

Howe, D. (2004), *St Peter's Catholic Primary School Leamington Spa 1879–2004: A Short History*, Leamington Spa

Kershaw, I. (1998), *Hitler 1889–1936: Hubris*, Penguin Press, London

May, T. (2011), *The Victorian Workhouse*, Shire Publications, Oxford

O'Shaughnessy, F. (1979), *A Spa and its Children*, Warwick Printing Company Ltd, Warwick

Saltzman, L.F. (1951), *A History of the County of Warwick*, Vol. 6: Knightlow Hundred, pp. 155–61: http://www.british-history. ac.uk/report.aspx?compid=57117 (date accessed: 11 March 2011)

Smith, B. (2001), *Warwickshire Tales of Mystery and Murder*, Countryside Books, Newbury

Wilson, A.N. (2005), *After the Victorians: 1901–1953*, Hutchinson, London

3 MILITARY SERVICE

1914

Ashworth, T. (2000), *Trench Warfare 1914–1918: The Live and Let Live System*, Macmillan Press, London

Baker, C. *The Long Trail: the British Army of 1914–1918* – http://www.1914-1918.net

Babington, A. (1986), *For the Sake of Example: Capital Courts Martial 1914–18*, Paladin Grafton Books, London

Brown, M. (2001), *The Western Front*, Pan Macmillan, London

—————— (2001), *Tommy Goes to War*, Tempus Publishing Ltd, Stroud

Corns, C. and Hughes-Wilson (2001), *Blindfold and Alone: British Military Executions in the Great War*, Cassell and Co., London

Doyle, P. (2010), *The British Soldier of the First World War*, Shire Publications, Oxford

Groom, W. (2003), *A Storm in Flanders*, Cassell, London

Holmes, R. (2005), *Tommy: The British Soldier on the Western Front 1914–1918*, Harper Perennial, London

Kershaw, I. (1998), *Hitler 1889–1936: Hubris*, Penguin Press, London

Macdonald, L. (1989), *1914, the Last Days of Hope*, Penguin Press, London

—————— (1991), *1914–1918: Voices and Images of the Great War*, Penguin Press, London

Strachan, H. (2006), *The First World War*, Simon and Schuster, London

Verhey, J.T. (1992), 'The Myth of Enthusiasm and the Rhetoric of Unity in Great War Germany', PhD thesis, University of California, Berkeley, in Williams, J. (2005), *Corporal Hitler and the Great War 1914–1918*, Frank Cass, Oxfordshire

Van Emden, R. (2002), *The Trench: Experiencing Life on the Front Line, 1916*, Bantam Press, London

Weber, T. (2010), *Hitler's First War*, Oxford University Press, Oxford

Williams, J. (2005), *Corporal Hitler and the Great War 1914–1918*, Frank Cass, Oxfordshire

Winter, D. (1979), *Death's Men: Soldiers of the Great War*, Penguin Press, Middlesex

DVD: *The Great War* (1964), Episode 5: 'This Business may last a long time', BBC

1915

Ashworth, T. (2000), *Trench Warfare 1914–1918: The Live and Let Live System*, Macmillan Press, London

Brown, M. (2001), *The Western Front*, Pan Macmillan, London

Gilbert, M. (2007), *Somme: The Heroism and Horror of War*, Hodder Headline, London

Groom, W. (2003), *A Storm in Flanders*, Cassell, London

Holmes, R. (2005), *Tommy: The British Soldier on the Western Front 1914–1918*, Harper Perennial, London

Keegan, J. (1983), *The Face of Battle: A Study of Agincourt, Waterloo and the Somme*, Penguin Books, London

Kershaw, I. (1998), *Hitler 1889–1936: Hubris*, Penguin Press, London

Macdonald, L. (1994), *1915, the Death of Innocence*, Headline Book Publishing, London

Weber, T. (2010), *Hitler's First War*, Oxford University Press, Oxford

Williams, J. (2005), *Corporal Hitler and the Great War 1914–1918*, Frank Cass, Oxfordshire

Winter, D. (1979), *Death's Men: Soldiers of the Great War*, Penguin Books, Middlesex

DVD: *The Great War* (1964), Episode 7: 'We Await the Heavenly Manna', BBC

1916

Ashurst, G. (1987), 'My Bit, Ramsbury' in Bird, A. and Bird, N. (eds) (2008), *Voices from the Front Line: Words from the Field of Human Conflict*, Summersdale Publishers Ltd, Chichester

Brown, M. (2001), *Tommy goes to War*, Tempus Publishing Ltd, Stroud
———— (2001), *The Western Front*, Pan Macmillan, London
———— (2002), *The Imperial War Museum Book of the Somme*, Pan Macmillan, London
Doyle, P. (2010), *The British Soldier of the First World War*, Shire Publications, Oxford
Gilbert, M. (2007), *Somme: The Heroism and Horror of War*, Hodder Headline, London
Holmes, R. (2005), *Tommy: The British Soldier on the Western Front 1914–1918*, Harper Perennial, London
Macdonald, L. (1993), *Somme*, Penguin Press, London
———— (1993), *The Roses of No Man's Land*, Penguin Press, London
Philpott, W. (2009), *Bloody Victory: The Sacrifice on the Somme*, Abacus, London
Weber, T. (2010), *Hitler's First War*, Oxford University Press, Oxford
Winter, D. (1979), *Death's Men: Soldiers of the Great War*, Penguin Books, Middlesex
DVD: *The Great War* (1964), Episode 13: 'The Devil is Coming', BBC

1917

Kershaw, I. (1998), *Hitler 1889–1936: Hubris*, Penguin Press, London
The Wartime Memories Project: www.wartimememoriesproject. com
Weber, T. (2010), *Hitler's First War*, Oxford University Press, Oxford
DVD: *The Great War* (1964), Episode 17: 'Surely we have Perished', BBC

1918

Brereton, J.M. and Savory, A.C.S. (1993), 'World War 1, 1918', *The History of the Duke of Wellingtons (West Riding) 1702–1992*, The Duke of Wellington's Regiment, Halifax

Brown, M. (2001), *The Western Front*, Pan Macmillan, London

Corns, C. and Hughes-Wilson, J. (2001), *Blindfold and Alone: British Military Executions in the Great War*, Cassell and Co., London

Holmes, R. (2005), *Tommy: The British Soldier on the Western Front 1914–1918*, Harper Perennial, London

Iron Duke (October 1933), the Duke of Wellington's Regiment (West Riding), Regimental Association Journal

Kershaw, I. (1998), *Hitler 1889–1936: Hubris*, Penguin Press, London

Persico, J. (2005), *11th Month, 11th Day, 11th Hour: Armistice Day 1918, World War One and its Violent Climax*, Arrow Books, London

Tolland, J. (1982), *No Man's Land*, Eyre Methuen, London

Weber, T. (2010), *Hitler's First War*, Oxford University Press, Oxford

Williams, J. (2005), *Corporal Hitler and the Great War 1914–1918*, Frank Cass, Oxfordshire

Wilson, A.N. (2005), *After the Victorians: 1901–1953*, Hutchinson, London

1919–26

www.westminster-abbey.org/ourhistory/people/unknown-warrior

4 RETURN TO CIVILIAN LIFE

Bolitho, P. (1997), *More Ripples from Warwickshire's Past*, self-published

Chapman, R. (2001), *Beyond their Duty: Heroes of the Green Howards*, The Green Howards Museum, Richmond

The Daily Telegraph, 28 July 1997 and 27 October 1997

Gilles, J. (1961), *The Ypres Salient*, Leo Cooper, London

Gliddon, G. (2000), *The Final Days 1918 (VCs of the First World War)*, Sutton Publishing, Stroud

Laffin, J. (1991), *The Western Front Illustrated 1914–1918*, Sutton Publishing Ltd, Stroud

www.oldcontemptibles.com

Ramsden, J. (2007), *Don't Mention the War: The British and the Germans since 1890*, Abacus, London

Smith, B. (2001), *Warwickshire Tales of Mystery and Murder*, Countryside Books, Newbury

www.triumph-herald.com

Yorkshire Post, 29 July 1997

5 THE STORY OF HENRY TANDEY AND HITLER

Brown, M. (2001), *The Western Front*, Pan Macmillan, London

www.cars-and-autos.info/triumph-cars/

Chamberlain Collection, University of Birmingham (NC 18/1/1046-1070)

Chapman, R. (2001), *Beyond their Duty: Heroes of the Green Howards*, The Green Howards Museum, Richmond

Charmley, J. (1989), *Chamberlain and the Lost Peace*, Hodder and Stoughton, Kent

Coventry Evening Telegraph, 29 July 1997

Gilles, J. (1961), *The Ypres Salient*, Leo Cooper, London

Kershaw, I. (1998), *Hitler 1889–1936: Hubris*, Penguin Press, London

Laffin, J. (1991), *The Western Front Illustrated 1914–1918*, Sutton Publishing, Stroud

Leamington Spa Courier, 23 December 1977

Marsh, P.T. (2010), *The Chamberlain Litany: Letters within a governing family from Empire to Appeasement*, Haus Publishing Ltd, London

Smith, B. (2001), *Warwickshire Tales of Mystery and Murder*, Countryside Books, Newbury

www.triumph-herald.com

Weber, T. (2010), *Hitler's First War*, Oxford University Press, Oxford

Williams, J. (2005), *Corporal Hitler and the Great War 1914–1918*, Frank Cass, Oxfordshire

Index